Third Edition

Islamic Studies

Level 2

Mansur Ahmad and Husain A. Nuri

weekend
Learning

ISBN: 978-0-9818483-5-8

First edition: 2008
Second edition: 2009
Third edition: 2010

Cover Design and Photography: Mansur Ahmad
Illustrations: Mansur Ahmad, Husain A. Nuri

Printed in China

WeekendLearning Publishers
5584 Boulder Crest St
Columbus, OH 43235
www.weekendlearning.com

Preface

The concept of a series of Islamic Studies books was conceived in 2002 when my brother and I were either teachers or principals of two weekend schools in two different states. We used several excellent textbooks or reference books for the schools. However, as teachers we found there was no single textbook available that could meet our classroom needs. Some of the available books had too many or too few lessons for an academic year. Some lessons were too long for a class hour, and some were too short. Some lessons were too difficult for the age or too basic for higher classes. Some books were written without a 12 year curriculum in mind. The lessons in higher grades, therefore, did not develop from the knowledge base of the prior years. Sometimes, extra emphasis was placed on one topic at the cost of other important topics. We thought a balanced knowledge base was, thus, lost.

We always felt there ought to be a way out. We began writing the lessons ourselves to meet the needs of our schools. We involved other teachers. For the next two years, we conducted classes based on the lessons we prepared. In the meantime, both of us met other principals and teachers across the country. We wanted to find out how they taught Islamic Studies and what their major concerns were. Most of the principals and teachers we talked to, expressed their inability to find or develop a good Islamic Studies curriculum. If they had a curriculum, they could not find lessons to complement it.

This survey prompted us to develop a functional, comprehensive Islamic Studies curriculum for weekend schools in the West. We wanted to have a curriculum that would include everything that Muslim students growing up in the West would ideally need to know. We wanted to include topics based on the life experiences of students growing up in the West. Muslim children growing up in the US, Europe and Australia are facing diverse challenges and conflicting pressures at schools and in friend circles. They are constantly influenced by the mainstream youth culture. We wanted lessons to address their issues from their perspective.

The curriculum alone would not be of any use unless there were lessons based on the curriculum. The lessons had to be age appropriate, and suitable for the typical class duration of most of the schools. As we continued to write and edit lessons over the next two years, we made the curriculum increasingly meaningful.

In 2007, we published pre-printed coil bound versions of these books. More than thirty schools in the US and UK used the books. We also received a large number of inquiries from many other schools. Based on the suggestions, comments and reviews received from many of these schools, we have edited the books and made changes as appropriate.

We are thankful to Allāh for giving us the ability to write these books. We pray to Allāh to accept our labor and make us successful in communicating the message of Islam. We hope Islamic schools and home schools in the USA and other countries will find these books useful. Any mistakes or errors in the books are our fault. We appreciate receiving meaningful comments and suggestions to improve the series.

"Our Rabb! Accept from us, you indeed are the all-Hearing, all-Knowing." (2:127)

January 15, 2008

Mansur Ahmad
Husain A. Nuri

Preface to the Second Edition

Alhamdulillah, the second edition of the book gives us the ability to improve upon the text, presentation and format without sacrificing the overall ease of use and appeal of the lessons. Each lesson now has two to three self-check review questions. We hope this will help reinforce learning. The self-check questions will refresh the students as they continue with the lesson. We have reformatted the homework section to make it user friendly.

We thank all the teachers and home-schooling parents for adopting this and other books in the series. We hope this edition, too, will receive similar recognition from weekend schools, teachers, students and parents. May Allāh accept our small effort.

May 15, 2009

Mansur Ahmad
Husain A. Nuri

Preface to the Third Edition

In the third edition of the book, we made small changes and improvements in the text. We retained all other features of the second edition, which was well accepted by parents, students and teachers.

As always, we thank Allāh for giving us time, resources and ability to continue working on this and other books in the series. Our special thank goes out to Sr. Oure Marvel for reading, commenting and sharing ideas to improve the book. Last, but not the least, we are thankful to all the teachers and home-schooling parents for adopting this and other books in the series. We hope this edition, too, will receive similar recognition from weekend schools, teachers, students and parents. May Allāh accept our small effort.

May 30, 2010

Mansur Ahmad
Husain A. Nuri

Table of Contents

How to Use this Book Effectively
Instructions for the Teacher and the Parents

The lessons for the second grade Islamic Studies are designed to develop and reinforce an understanding of the five pillars of Islam. Along with that, the students are also introduced to some of the values of Islam. As with other books in the series, this book, too, starts with a few topics on Allāh (swt), the Qur'ān and the Hadīth. Short biographies of several prophets are introduced as a foundation from which future lessons are developed.

The teachers are encouraged to read the lesson before coming to the class. Most of the lessons can be read out to the students. At this age students love listening to story type presentations. Each lesson in this grade starts with a coloring section. The purpose of this section is to help the students compose themselves before teaching starts. Students should be given about 10 minutes to complete the coloring. A word of appreciation or encouragement, insha-Allāh, will improve the attention of the class. If the teacher sits close to the students, and at a similar height to the chairs of the students, s/he might be able to draw more attention. Please avoid speaking in a monotonous voice. Rather, change the voice from loud to whispers as appropriate. Use body language and other gestures, such as, using your hands to show a flying bird when you are teaching "Allah created all the birds." Be creative in teaching! Make frequent eye contact with the students. Ask questions frequently to reinforce learning.

For maximum benefit, each lesson should be completed in one class hour. We recommend that a test be conducted after every fifth or sixth lesson. Weekend Learning has designed an Excel based user friendly program to record homework and exam scores. It will become handy when report cards are prepared. For this program as well as question bank, ready to print exam and homework questions, please obtain a CD from the publisher.

Homework:

Teachers are requested to assign regular homework and also grade these regularly. For this grade, the time commitment for homework is about 10 minutes per lesson. It is strongly encouraged that parents work with the student for the homework. A regular supervision of homework by a parent will indicate that education is valued.

Teaching Respect:

From an early age, students should be taught to show respect to Allāh, His Prophets, Angels and the Companions. The teachers and parents are requested to mention the following:

Whenever the word Allāh appears in the book, please add the glorification "Subhāna-hu wa-Ta'ālā."

Whenever the word Muhammad, or other words indicating Muhammad, e.g. Rasulullah, the Prophet, or Nabi appears, please add the prayer, "Salla-llāhu 'alaihi wa Sallam." We have used (S) in the book to prompt the prayer. Whenever the student comes across the names of a prophet or an angel, please add the prayer "Alai-hi-s Salām". This is noted by (A). The students should be taught to add the prayer "Radi-allāhu 'an-hu" for a khalifa or a male companion of the Prophet (S). For a woman companion, the prayer "Radi-allāhu 'an-hā" should be used. These are noted by (R) or (ra).

Suggestions:

Please provide suggestions, corrections, ideas, etc., to improve the book by sending an e-mail to the publisher at weekendLearning@gmail.com. It is a combined effort of the publisher, authors, teachers and parents to prepare our future ummah. May Allāh guide us all! Amin.

Allah (swt): *Our Creator*

Assalamu alaikum. Welcome to the class. Let us start by coloring this Arabic word. The word says: Allahu.

Allah **subhanahu wa ta'āla** is our creator. The word "subhanahu wa ta'āla" means "**Glory** to Him, the High." Whenever we say Allah's name, we should say subhanahu wa ta'āla to honor Him. We say it to show our respect. In English we write (**swt**) to remind us to say subhanahu wa ta'āla.

Allah (swt) created the heavens and the earth. If you look at the sky on a clear night, you will see thousands of stars. Allah (swt) created all of them.

Allah (swt) created the angels, **jinn**, and also all human beings. He also created **Iblis**, who does the bad things. We cannot see angels or jinn, but Allah (swt) can see them.

Allah (swt) created everything in the **universe**. He created everything to help us. For example, Allah (swt) created the sun to help us. Without the sun nothing in the world could live and grow. Allah (swt) created air for us. Without clean air, we could not live even for a minute. Allah (swt) created water for us. We need water everyday. Our bodies are even made with water.

Allah (swt) created everything in the best way. He created the living things in pairs. He created many types of living things. There are so many types of insets, birds, fishes, plants, and fruits.

We cannot finish counting all of the creations of Allah (swt). If we get thousands of pens, we still could not write all the things that Allah (swt) created.

	Write one thing that Allah (swt) created in the sky:
	Write one living thing that Allah (swt) created:
	Write one thing that Allah (swt) created to help us:

Allah (swt) created elephants and giant dinosaurs. When you see a butterfly, remember that Allah (swt) created it. Only Allah (swt) can create. Nobody else can create. Some people worship **idols**, but idols cannot create anything.

If we are at school, we cannot be at home at the same time. We can be in only one place at a time. Allah (swt) is everywhere at the same time. He is both inside and outside of everything.

Allah (swt) sees us all the time, but we cannot see Him. He is not a man. He is not a woman. He has no parents, and no children. Nobody made Allah (swt), but Allah (swt) made everything.

What did Allah (swt) create?

How many things did the idols create?

If we want, can we see Allah (swt)?

Let us look out a window. Everything in nature that we see is created by Allah (swt). He created the birds, trees, green grass, colorful flowers, and fruits. Allah (swt) also created the rocks and sand. Next time you see a river or a mountain, think of who made it.

Allah (swt) gives us food, drink and everything that we need. So, we should say *Thank you* to Allah (swt). We can say thanks by doing what Allah (swt) wants us to do. We can make salah, fast during Ramadan, and be good to other people.

Today, on your way back home, look out your car windows. See how many things Allah (swt) made in this world.

Draw and color the other half of the flower

Words that I learned today:

Subhanahu wa Ta'āla   • Glory   • (swt) • Jinn • Iblis • Universe
Idols • Salah • Ramadan •

1. In these four ovals, write any four things that Allah (swt) created.

2. Fill in the blanks with the right word from the box:

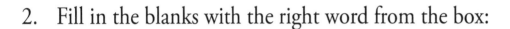

create   everything   family   Ramadan   thank you

Allah (swt) has no _____.

We should always say _____ to Allah (swt).

Allah (swt) created _____.

We fast during _____.

Idols cannot _____ anything.

3. Who is our Creator?

_____

4. Inside this box, draw a picture of something that Allah (swt) created.

5. Everything that we can make comes from something that Allah (swt) gave us. Circle only those things that we can make using something Allah (swt) created.

Rain	House	Mountains	Cars	Sun
Horse	Stars	Playground	Trees	Grass
Pencil	Flower	Books	Apple	River

Blessings of Allah (swt)

Assalamu alaikum. Welcome to the class. Let us start by coloring these fruits. All these are blessings of Allah (swt).

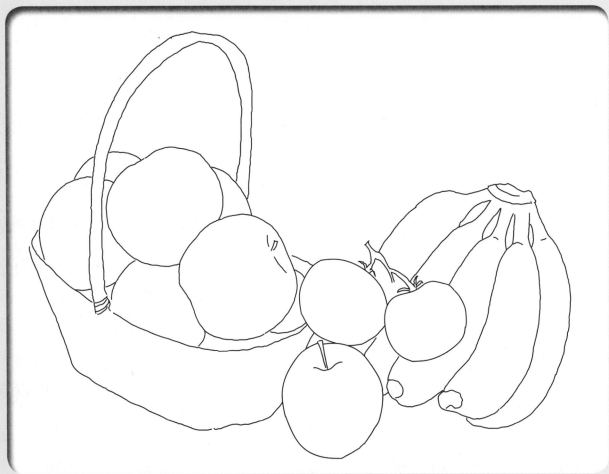

Allah (swt) is most-Merciful. Merciful means to be kind, caring, and forgiving. Because Allah (swt) is most-Merciful, one of His names is **Ar-Rahman**. He has another name, **Ar-Rahim**, which means He is most-Kind.

Allah (swt) is so kind that He gives His **blessings** to everybody. People who do not believe in Allah (swt) still get some blessings. Those who believe, get much more blessings. Allah (swt) gives us many gifts. Not all these gifts are in a colorful box. Let us learn about some of these gifts.

Let us start from our faces. Allah (swt) gave us two eyes, so that we can see. The eyes are wonderful gifts from Allah (swt). He gave us a nose, so that we can smell. He gave us ears, so that we can hear. He gave us skin, so that we can feel. He gave us a brain, so that we can think. These are all gifts from Allah (swt). These gifts are His blessings to us.

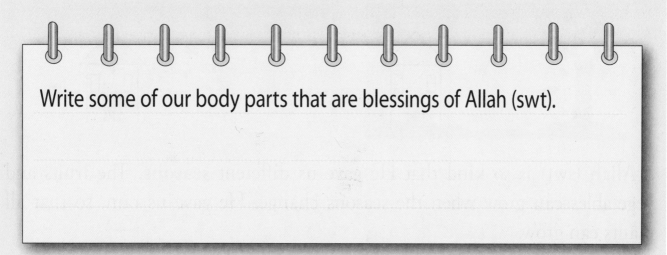

Write some of our body parts that are blessings of Allah (swt).

Do you remember how little you were last year? This year, you are bigger and taller. Allah (swt) made you big and tall. It is a blessing from Allah (swt) that we grow up. He gave us life and He gave us our families. These all are blessings of Allah (swt).

Allah (swt) gave us all kinds of food. He gave us different fruits, vegetables, fishes and meats. How many blessings can we count? We cannot finish counting them! Everyone gets some blessings from Allah (swt).

Allah (swt) is so kind that He gave us day and night. The night is for sleeping and the day is for working. If there were no daylight, then the world would be dark and cold. Everything would be **frozen**. If there were no night time, then the world would be too hot. The world would be drier than a **desert**.

Allah (swt) is so kind that He gave us different **seasons**. The fruits and vegetables can grow when the seasons change. He gave us rain, so that all plants can grow.

	Write any two blessings that everyone gets.
◯	Write how rain is a blessing.

If we become sick, Allah (swt) makes us better. He takes away our pain. If we make mistakes and we say sorry to Allah (swt), He **forgives** us. This is a big gift to us.

Allah (swt) taught us how to speak, read and write. Allah (swt) made us better than the animals.

Allah (swt) is so kind that He gave us the Qur'an and sent us our Prophet Muhammad (S). The Qur'an is a blessing for the people. Our Prophet (S) is a blessing for the whole world. We love Prophet Muhammad (S) very much.

Words that I learned today:

Blessings • Frozen • Desert • Seasons • Forgive • Ar-Rahman • Ar-Rahim

1. Fill in the blanks using the words from this box.

    | gifts | count | Ar-Rahman | kind | forgives |

    Allah (swt) _____ us if we say sorry for our mistakes.

    The name _____ means most-Kind.

    We cannot _____ all the blessings from Allah (swt).

    Allah (swt) is very _____ to us.

    Allah (swt) gives us so many _____.

2. In the ovals, write any four blessings Allah (swt) gave you.

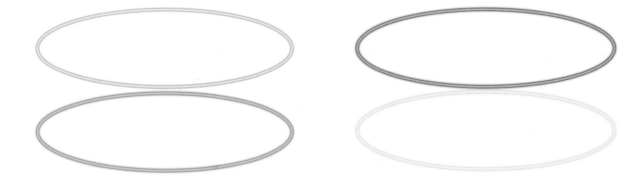

3. Unscramble these letters to make words. (All these words are from the **Words That I learned Today** box)

SRETED   D __ __ __ __ __

GFVOERI   F __ __ __ __ __ __

MHRANA   R __ __ __ __ __

SOSNEAS   S __ __ __ __ __ __

4. Circle **Yes** if it is correct, and circle **No** if it is wrong.

Allah (swt) is mean.	YES	NO
Allah (swt) gives us all kinds of food.	YES	NO
Allah (swt) makes us better when we are sick.	YES	NO
Allah (swt) did not give us blessings.	YES	NO
Allah (swt) gave us eyes, ears, nose and mouth.	YES	NO

The Qur'an

Assalamu alaikum. Welcome to the class. Let us start by coloring this Qur'an and its stand (rehal).

The Qur'an is a Book of Allah (swt). All the words that you see in the Qur'an are from Allah (swt). It was not written by Prophet Muhammad (S) or by other people. The Qur'an is written in Arabic.

Hundreds of years ago, in a month of Ramadan, Prophet Muhammad (S) was spending a night in a cave near Makkah. Alone in the cave, Prophet Muhammad (S) was thinking how to help his people.

In that night of Ramadan, angel **Jibril** (A) came to the cave and brought a few sentences or **verses** of the Qur'an. The sentences of the Qur'an are called **Ayat** or **signs**. For the next many years, Jibril (A) kept on bringing a few verses or small parts of the Qur'an. After 23 years, the Qur'an was complete.

Whenever Prophet Muhammad (S) received verses of the Qur'an, first he memorized them. Then he asked his followers to write them down.

The Qur'an has 114 chapters. A chapter of the Qur'an is called a **surah**. Some surahs are long, some are quite short. Some surahs came to Prophet (S) when he was in Makkah. Some surahs came when he was in Madinah. We can also divide the Qur'an into 30 parts or **juz**. This is done for easy reading.

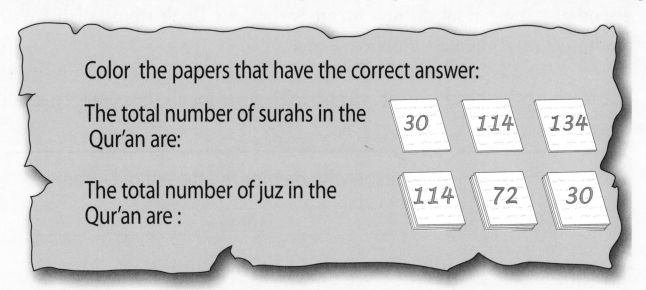

Color the papers that have the correct answer:

The total number of surahs in the Qur'an are: 30 114 134

The total number of juz in the Qur'an are : 114 72 30

The Qur'an is a Book for all people. It is a guide for us. It tells us to follow the **Right Path.** It tells us not to do bad things.

Every word in the Qur'an today is the same as it came to Prophet Muhammad (S). Not a single word of the Qur'an has changed in the last 1400 years. Allah (swt) saves it from any changes.

Many Muslims memorize every ayat of the Qur'an. A person who memorizes the entire Qur'an is called a **Hafiz**. We read parts of the Qur'an in our daily salah. All of us should memorize at least some surahs from the Qur'an.

Some Muslims do not fully understand Arabic. They try to understand the Qur'an by reading in Arabic and using **translations**. Translation means reading the original book in another language. The best way to read and understand the Qur'an is in Arabic. When the Qur'an is **recited**, we should listen carefully and quietly.

Allah (swt) gave us His complete **message** in the Qur'an. Allah (swt) will not send any more Books. The Qur'an is the Last Book from Allah (swt). Muhammad (S) is the Last Prophet.

The teachings of the Qur'an are the best. They are for all the people from all over the world.

A _____ is a person who memorized the entire Qur'an.

Some surahs came in _____ , some in _____ .

Will Allah (swt) send any other book after the Qur'an? _____ .

Words that I learned today:

Jibril • Verses • Ayat • Ramadan • Surah • Juz • Right Path • Hafiz • Translation • Recite • Message •

1. Draw lines from left to right to complete the sentences. One example is shown for you.

The teachings of the Qur'an   the Right Path.

It took 23 years   chapters

The Quran has 114   are the best.

The Qur'an shows us   written in Arabic.

The Qur'an is   to complete the Qur'an.

2. Mark with a ☑ if it is correct. Mark with an ☒ if it is wrong.

Allah (swt) sent two more books after the Qur'an. ☐

The Qur'an is only for the Imam to read. ☐

It took 1400 years to complete the Qur'an. ☐

Translations of the Qur'an are in many languages. ☐

The Qur'an is the best book from Allah (swt). ☐

3. A chapter in the Qur'an is called: (Color the correct oval)

Ramadan   Jibril   Surah

4. The number of chapters in the Qur'an are: (Color the correct oval)

23   114   400

5. The number of Juz in the Qur'an are: (Color the correct oval)

23   30   93

6. Allah (swt) sent the Qur'an in: (Color the correct oval)

Arabic   Persian   English

7. Fill in the blanks with the right word from the box.

listen   teachings   last   words

All the _____ in the Qur'an are from Allah (swt).

When the Qur'an is recited, we should _____ to it carefully.

Prophet Muhammad (S) is the _____ Prophet.

The _____ of the Qur'an are the best.

Prophet Muhammad (S)

Assalamu alaikum. Welcome to the class. Let us start by coloring the word Muhammad (S).

Prophet Muhammad (**Salla Allahu 'alaihi wa Sallam**) is the last prophet or **Nabi** for all the people of the world. Salla Allahu 'alaihi wa Sallam means 'May Allah's Blessings and Peace be upon him'. We may write this as (S).

About 1400 years ago, Muhammad (S) was born in Makkah, a town in Arabia. His father was **Abdullah** and his mother was **Aminah**. Abdullah died before Muhammad (S) was born.

In those days in Arabia, a nurse-mother would feed and take care of a baby. Aminah sent her new born baby Muhammad (S) with a nurse-mother for a few years. The nurse-mother was very loving. She took Muhammad (S) to her far-away home. She took good care of him.

A few years later, Muhammad (S) came back to live with his mother. After about a year, Aminah passed away. Muhammad (S) was only six years old at that time. His grandfather was very kind, and took care of Muhammad (S) for two years. Then the grandfather also passed away. Muhammad (S) then lived with an uncle.

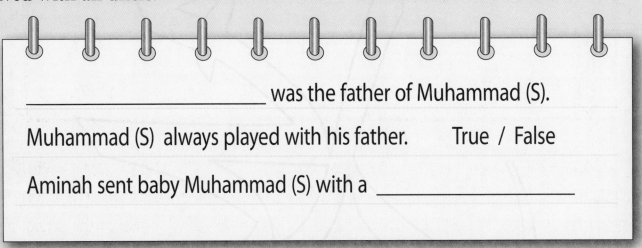

_____ was the father of Muhammad (S).

Muhammad (S) always played with his father.   True / False

Aminah sent baby Muhammad (S) with a _____

Even from his childhood, Muhammad (S) always spoke the truth. People called him **Al-Amin**, because they trusted him. He was a bright and honest person. When he was a young man, he worked for a rich woman named **Khadijah**. He took care of her business. She was so happy with his work that she married him.

Many people in Makkah were bad. They were mean to the poor and to the women. Muhammad (S) did not like this. He used to go to a cave to think about these problems. One night in the month of Ramadan, angel Jibril (A) came to him with five ayat from Allah (swt). Muhammad (S) became a **Rasulullah**, or a Prophet of Allah. For the next 23 years, angel Jibril brought parts of the Qur'an to Prophet Muhammad (S).

Prophet Muhammad (S) told his people about the words of Allah (swt). At first, only a few people believed him and became Muslim. Many people did not believe him. They were hard on him. Some of them wanted to kill him. As he could not teach Islam in Makkah, he moved to Madinah. Here people loved him very much. He could freely teach Islam in Madinah.

When Prophet Muhammad (S) was in Madinah, bad people from Makkah came to fight with him. They were angry because he was teaching Islam. They fought many times, but could not defeat the Muslims in any battle.

Khadijah was the _____ of Muhammad (S).

Jibril (A) brought parts of the Qur'an for _____ years.

After many years, Prophet (S) came back to Makkah. The people in Makkah were afraid. They thought Prophet Muhammad (S) would punish them for fighting against the Muslims. Prophet Muhammad (S) was very kind and forgiving. He did not punish anybody. He forgave all the people in Makkah. People liked his kindness. People of Makkah then became Muslim.

Prophet Muhammad (S) was the best person. We love him very much. He was not a king. He was a servant of Allah (swt) and the Last Prophet. We are all servants of Allah (swt) too. When our dear Rasulullah (S) was 63 years old, he passed away.

Words that I learned today:

Prophet • Salla Allahu 'alaihi wa Sallam • Nabi • Abdullah •
Aminah • Al-Amin • Khadijah • Rasulullah •

1. Muhammad (S) was called Al-Amin because people: (Color the correct box.)

| Hated him | Trusted him | Went to school with him |

2. When Rasulullah (S) was 63 years old, he: (Color the correct oval)

| Passed away | Became a king | Married Khadijah |

3. The Qur'an was sent to Prophet Muhammad (S) over a period of: (Color the correct triangle)

| 63 years | 100 years | 23 years |

4. What does "Salla Allahu 'alaihi wa Sallam" mean?

_____

_____

5. These flashlights show six events in the life of Prophet Muhammad (S). Sort these flashlights in the correct order. The 6th flashlight is already marked for you.

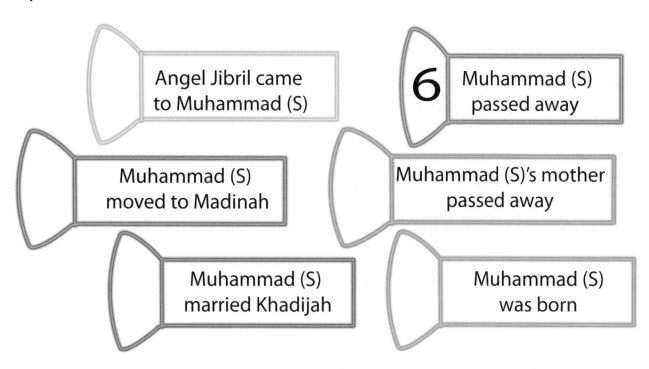

6. Write the four different names or titles of Muhammad (S). These names are in the **Words I Learned Today** box.

1. _____

2. _____

3. _____

4. _____

Hadith and Sunnah

Assalamu alaikum. Welcome to the class. Let us start by coloring the six books of hadith.

Prophet Muhammad (S) lived hundreds of years before we were born. When the Prophet (S) was alive, many people carefully listened to him and watched his actions. They used to tell others about the Prophet (S), and what he said or did. The sayings and actions of the Prophet (S) are known as a **Hadith**. The doings or the way Rasulullah (S) lived and worked are called the **Sunnah**.

Many people memorized the teachings of the Prophet (S). They passed on these teachings to their children and grandchildren.

As time passed, many people in the world became Muslim. But they had never seen the Prophet (S). They wanted to know what Prophet Muhammad (S) said or what he did. They learned about the life of the Prophet (S) through people who had seen him. After many years, the people who had seen the Prophet (S) also passed away. People thought that they would slowly forget what the Prophet (S) did or said. They began to write down what they remembered.

A wise person named **Imam al-Bukhari** collected the **ahadith** that people remembered. More than one hadith are called ahadith. Imam al-Bukhari spent all his life collecting ahadith. He traveled to distant places and met people who knew hadith. Some people told him false hadith that the Prophet (S) did not say. Imam al-Bukhari was wise to find out which ahadith were correct and which were false. He collected only the correct hadith. His collections are known as correct or **Sahih**. His book is called Sahih Bukhari.

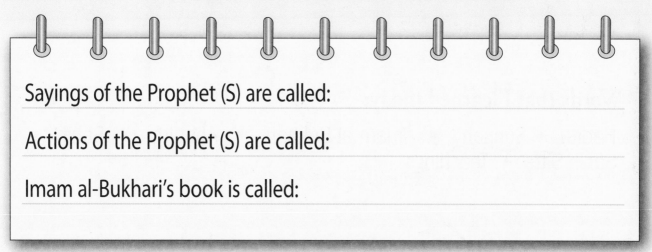

Sayings of the Prophet (S) are called:

Actions of the Prophet (S) are called:

Imam al-Bukhari's book is called:

After Imam al-Bukhari, five other Imams also collected hadith. With their five books and Sahih Bukhari, we have a total of six books of ahadith. These six books are known as **Sahih Sitta** or the "True Six". Look at page 30. Can you name some of the collectors of ahadith?

The Qur'an is the most important book in Islam. The Hadith books are the second most important books. Ahadith give details about many Islamic laws. For example, the Qur'an tells us to give zakat and charity. How much do we give in zakat? The ahadith give us the details.

Hadith tells us how our Prophet (S) lived, and how people of his time lived. Hadith books have many good teachings about how to lead our lives. Our dear Prophet Muhammad (S) is not with us, but we can learn about him from the hadith books.

Hadith helps us with the details of Islamic laws.	True / False
After Imam Bukhari how many Imams collected hadith? _____	
What does Sahih Sitta mean? _____	

Words that I learned today:

Hadith • Sunnah • Imam al-Bukhari • Ahadith • Sahih • Sahih Sitta • Teachings •

1. Draw lines to match a word to its correct meaning.

Ahadith   "True Six"

Sunnah   Words or actions of the Prophet(S)

Sahih Sitta   Collector of Hadith

Hadith   The way Rasulullah lived

Al-Bukhari   More than one Hadith

2.   Why did people write down the words and actions of the Prophet (S)? Circle all the choices that are correct.

A.   They wanted to know how the Prophet (S) lived and worked.

B.   People thought Hadith would be lost unless they wrote them down.

C.   People wanted to pass time by writing books.

D.   People wanted to slowly forget the Prophet (S).

3. Circle **T** for true if the sentence is correct, circle **F** for false if the sentence is wrong.

The six hadith books are called the "Sahih Saba."   T   F

Imam al-Bukhari collected many ahadith.   T   F

The word ahadith means one hadith.   T   F

The Five Pillars of Islam

Assalamu alaikum. Welcome to the class. Let us start by coloring these five pillars of a house.

Have you ever built a **sandcastle** on a beach? Every time a wave of water comes, it washes the sandcastle away. To make a strong house or a castle, we need many **pillars**. The pillars hold up the roof and give support to the walls. They support the house. The pillars should be very strong, made of bricks, wood, or steel. Without strong pillars, a house will fall down.

The religion of Islam is like a house. It has five pillars. These pillars make the religion strong. These are not pillars of wood or bricks. These pillars tell us what we should do to be good Muslims. These pillars are the five basic duties of all Muslims. If we do not follow these pillars, our lives will be in a mess. A good Muslim cares for the five pillars in his or her life. In the next few weeks, we will insha-Allah learn more about these five pillars. Today we will learn their names and short meanings.

1. The first pillar is **Shahadah**. It means we believe there is no god but Allah, and that Muhammad (S) is His prophet.

2. The second pillar is **Salah**. These are the five daily prayers. Salah is done five times a day alone or in a group. Men and women, boys and girls should make salah. Women and girls can join the group salah whenever possible.

Without pillars a house _____ down.

The first pillar of Islam is _____

3. The third pillar is **Sawm** or **Fasting**. It means that during the month of Ramadan, grown-up Muslims do not eat or drink during daytime. Fasting helps us increase our faith in Allah (swt).

4. The fourth pillar is **Zakah** or **charity**. It means we give part of our money to the needy people. If a person has savings and wealth, he or she has to pay zakah. If a person does not have wealth or savings, there is no need to pay zakah. Rich people cannot receive zakah from others.

The second pillar of Islam is _____

The fourth pillar of Islam is _____

5. The fifth pillar is **Hajj**. It means going to Makkah in the month of Hajj. During Hajj, a person has to visit the Kabah do several other duties. If we can, we have to make Hajj at least once in our lifetime.

Can you write the names of the five pillars below?

	1.
	2.
	3.
	4.
	5.

Words that I learned today:

Sandcastle • Pillars • Shahadah • Salah • Sawm • Fasting • Zakah • Charity • Hajj •

1. Look for the following words in the Word Find puzzle.

| PILLARS | SHAHADAH | SALAH | ZAKAH |
| CHARITY | SAWM | HAJJ | ISLAM |

```
A G W Z S E O C
S H A H A D A H
A D G O W E T A
L C O M M P K R
A N Z A K A H I
H A J J U S E T
I S L A M W M Y
A P I L L A R S
```

2. The second pillar of Islam is: (Color the correct oval)

Salah   Sawm   Hajj

3. Zakah means: (Color the correct oval)

Fasting   Charity   Praying

4. Two pillars do not have names. Can you write the missing names?

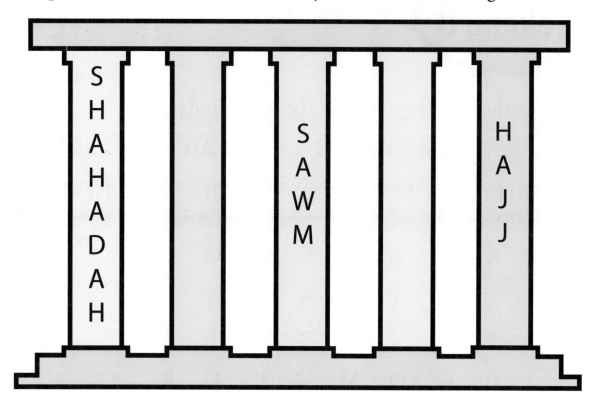

5. Fill in the blanks using the words from the box.

Shahadah   Salah   Sawm   Hajj   five

We should make _____ at least once in our life.

The first pillar of Islam is _____.

The five daily prayers is _____.

Fasting or _____ means not eating or drinking from sunrise to sunset every day during Ramadan.

Islam has _____ pillars.

Shahadah: *The First Pillar*

Assalamu alaikum. Welcome to the class. Let us color the following words.

No deity but one Allah

There is only one god, Allah (swt). He is our Master. He created us. We are always in need of Allah (swt). We **worship** only Allah (swt).

We do not worship anyone else. Nobody else created us. Nobody can help us the way Allah (swt) helps us. Allah (swt) is the only **deity**. A deity is one whom we worship.

Allah (swt) had sent many prophets. All the prophets taught Islam as the only religion. Prophet Muhammad (S) taught us the complete Islam. He showed us how to lead our lives. Allah (swt) sent us the Qur'an through prophet Muhammad (S). Our Prophet (S) has passed away. But the Qur'an remains with us. When we believe in Prophet Muhammad (S), we believe in the Qur'an that came through him.

We are Muslim because we believe that Allah (swt) is the only God, and Muhammad (S) is His Last Prophet. In Arabic, we say:

**Ash-hadu an la ilaha illal-lahu
wa ash-hadu anna Muhammadur Rasulullah**

Shahadah has two parts. The first part reminds us that Allah (swt) is only One. The second part says that Muhammad (S) is His Rasul or prophet.

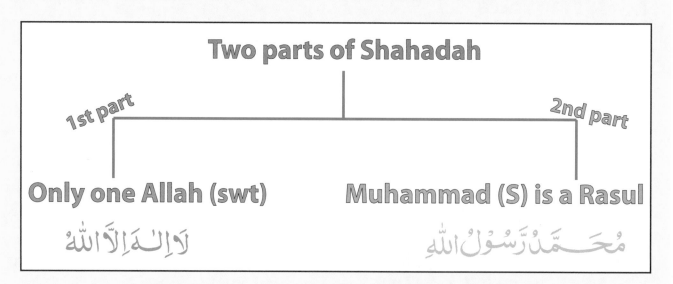

La ilaha illal-lahu: This is the first part of Shahadah. This part declares that there is no other deity but Allah (swt). Allah (swt) is the Only Deity. This means we can only worship Allah (swt).

Muhammadur Rasulullah: This is the second part of Shahadah. This part declares that Muhammad (S) is the Prophet or **Rasul** of Allah (swt). We follow the teachings of Muhammad (S), but worship only Allah (swt).

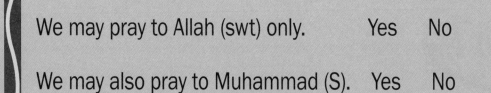

We may pray to Allah (swt) only.　　　Yes　　No

We may also pray to Muhammad (S).　Yes　　No

Together "**Ash-hadu an la ilaha illal-lahu wa ash-hadu anna Muhammadur Rasulullah**" is called the Shahadah. Shahadah means to give **witness**. We can give witness when we know something clearly. Muslims clearly know there is no deity but Allah (swt). As Muslims, we must say the Shahadah and believe in it. When a non-Muslim person wants to become Muslim, he or she says Shahadah.

We do not worship Prophet Muhammad (S). He was a rasul. A rasul is a person who brings messages from Allah (swt). Prophet Muhammad (S) brought the Qur'an. We believe in all the messages in the Qur'an.

No deity but ALLAH

Words that I learned today:

Worship • Deity • La ilaha illal-lahu Muhammadur Rasulullah • Rasul • Witness •

1. Write **Yes** if correct, Write **No** if wrong.

More prophets will come after Prophet Muhammad (S). _____

We may worship two gods. _____

We do not worship Prophet Muhammad (S). _____

2. Search the following words in the puzzle.

| RASUL | WORSHIP | WITNESS | DEITY | SHAHADAH | ISLAM |

R	U	E	D	Y	O	P	M	S
W	O	R	S	H	I	P	I	H
D	J	A	S	A	S	I	E	A
C	V	S	H	W	L	I	K	H
I	L	U	S	A	A	N	F	A
H	K	L	R	S	M	B	M	D
J	W	I	T	N	E	S	S	A
K	A	N	E	T	G	D	U	H
D	E	I	T	Y	A	I	P	D

3. Mark with a ☑ if it is correct. Mark with an ☒ if it is wrong.

We worship both Allah (swt) and ProphetMuhammad (S). ☐

The Shahadah means to give witness. ☐

Allah(swt) is the only deity. ☐

Prophet Muhammad (S) was a rasul of Allah (swt). ☐

Prophet Muhammad (S) taught the complete Islam. ☐

We can be Muslim without believing in Shahadah. ☐

4. Memorize the Shahadah. Be ready to recite it in front of your teacher next week!

Salah: *The Second Pillar*

Assalamu alaikum. Welcome to the class. Let us color the area of a masjid where an Imam stands to lead the salah.

Salah is the second pillar of Islam. Salah or prayer is done five times every day. These prayers are done at their own set times. All Muslims, young or old, men or women, must make salah. It is a duty for us.

The names and times of the five salah are as follows:

1. Fajr: at early morning, after dawn and before sunrise,

2. Dhuhr: just after noon time,

3. Asr: mid-afternoon,

4. Maghrib: right after sunset,

5. 'Isha: evening, some time after the Maghrib salah.

Fajr   Dhuhr   Asr   Maghrib   'Isha

We can make these five salah alone or with a group of people. Some salah must be done along with other people. On Fridays, we make salah in a group. This is Salatul **Jumuah**. When we pray Salatul Jumuah, we do not pray Salatul Dhuhr. On the days of Eid, we make salah in group. Many people attend the Eid salah.

Salah brings us closer to Allah (swt). Making salah on time shows that we have faith in Allah (swt) and we follow Islam.

Do you know why the time of salah is spread out over the day? It is because a Muslim should remember Allah (swt) all day, even between their jobs or games. Dhuhr prayer is right in the middle of school or work hours. During the work hours we should not forget Allah (swt). Similarly, during the afternoon or other busy times, we should not forget Allah (swt).

Other than the five daily salah, we can make extra salah. It is good for us to make these extra salah. These extra salah are made before or after the five daily salah.

Before salah, we should make **wudu**. Wudu means we have to wash our faces, hands, and wipe our heads and feet. Sometimes we may have to take a shower too! We should not pray with dirty clothes.

Before salah, a call is made for prayer. This call is the **Adhan**, and it is done in a nice, **melodious** voice. The Adhan is a reminder that it is time for salah. Do you know the words of the Adhan? The words of adhan are easy to remember, and you can learn them quickly. Then you can be a **muadhdhin** in your home, which means you call for the prayer!

You may make salah alone, but it is better to make salah in a group. When you are in a group, an **Imam** leads the salah. The Imam is the leader of the salah. The Imam stands in front and all others stand behind him in straight lines. During salah, we face towards the **Ka'bah** in Makkah. This direction is called the **Qiblah**.

We should make salah at their set times. We may pray salah in any clean place. Whenever you hear someone calling to salah, leave your games or work, and join the salah. Allah (swt) **accepts** the salah and rewards us for praying.

Words that I learned today:

Salah • Jumuah • Wudu • Adhan • Melodious • Muadhdhin • Imam • Ka'bah • Qiblah • Accept •

Steps of Salah

Stand for salāt facing the direction of the Ka'bah.

Front and side view

Raise hands for takbir. Fold them back to recite sūrahs.

Bend down for ruku.

Front and side view

Stand up from ruku.

Bow down to make sujud.

Sit down from sujud, jalsa position.

Front, side and back view

Second sujud from jalsa position.

At the end of 2nd raka'at, sit down after 2nd sujud to recite tashahud.

Complete salāt - turn face first to the right and then to the left for salam.

1. Write the names of the five prayers in the order they are prayed in a day.

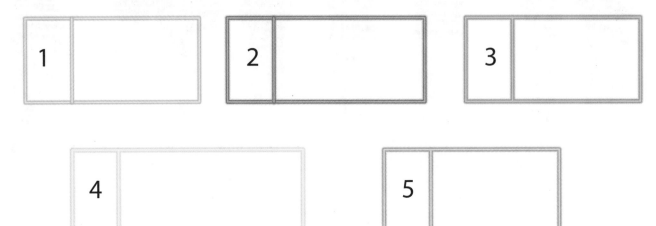

2. Fill in the blanks using the words from this box.

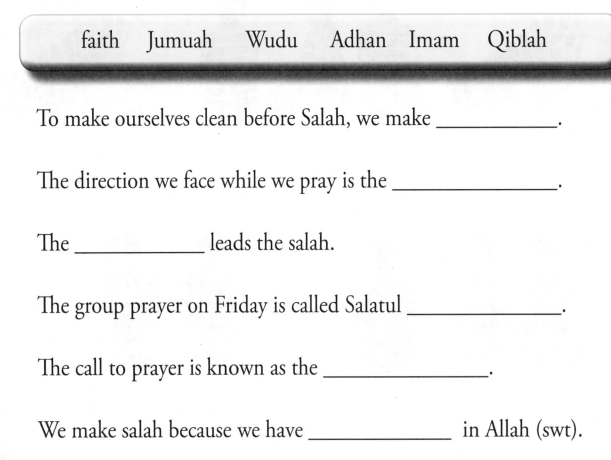

faith   Jumuah   Wudu   Adhan   Imam   Qiblah

To make ourselves clean before Salah, we make _____.

The direction we face while we pray is the _____.

The _____ leads the salah.

The group prayer on Friday is called Salatul _____.

The call to prayer is known as the _____.

We make salah because we have _____ in Allah (swt).

3. Match the names of the five salah to the correct times with a line.

Fajr   right after sunset

Dhuhr   mid-afternoon

Asr   after dawn and before sunrise

Maghrib   at night

'Isha   right after noon time

4. Search the following words in the puzzle.

SALAH   JUMUAH   ADHAN   IMAM

QIBLAH   ACCEPT   PRAY   KABAH

```
S  J  U  M  U  A  H
A  I  M  A  M  M  U
L  A  P  R  A  Y  A
A  C  C  E  P  T  D
H  D  H  D  H  I  H
Q  I  B  L  A  H  A
N  K  A  B  A  H  N
```

5. extra**credit.** In the puzzle, you have not used some of the letters. With these unused letters, write the title of the one who calls the adhan.

_____

Sawm: *The Third Pillar*

Assalamu alaikum. Welcome to the class. This is Imran's Iftar, after his first day of fasting. Let us color the drawing to make it look yummy.

The third pillar of Islam is **Sawm**. A simple meaning of Sawm is fasting. Fasting means to stay away from eating or drinking. When Muslims fast, they do not eat or drink from **dawn** to sunset.

Fasting is done in the month of **Ramadan**. It is the ninth month of Islamic calendar. The month of Ramadan starts when we see a new moon. The month also ends when we see another new moon.

Fasting brings us closer to Allah (swt). During Ramadan Muslims pray more and read more chapters of the Qur'an. At the masjid or at home we make a special salah at night. This salah is called **Tarawih**.

Since fasting starts at dawn, we may eat before dawn. Your parents may get up early in the morning, well before breakfast time, to eat some food. They will not eat anything throughout the day. If you have fasted, you know that you cannot even drink water during the daytime.

When the sun sets, it is time to break the fast. At that time you eat and drink good food. Your breakfast is at sunset! This meal is called **Iftar**.

The special salat in Ramadan is called: _____

Ramadan is the _____ month in Islamic calendar.

We break our fast with a meal called: _____

Fasting shows us ways to **worship** Allah (swt). Fasting is for our benefit. Allah (swt) rewards those who fast during the month of Ramadan. As you grow older, you should try to fast more days. In a few years, you will be able to fast the entire month of Ramadan!

Ramadan is the month to receive more blessings, mercy and forgiveness from Allah's (swt). To receive these blessings, we should fast, pray and remember Allah (swt) a lot. We should stay away from all bad actions.

If you are sick, or traveling, you may skip fasting. Later you will have to make up the days that you missed.

Ramadan is the month when the Qur'an started to come to Prophet Muhammad (S). Ramadan is a blessed month. When Ramadan ends, the happy day of **Eid al-Fitr** arrives. We should not fast on this day. We should thank Allah (swt) for the month of Ramadan. We should enjoy the day of Eid with our friends and families. We should share our food with the people who do not have enough.

We enjoy Eid before Ramadan starts.	True / False
A sick person or traveler may skip fasting.	True / False
In Ramadan Allah(swt) sends blessings, mercy and _____	

Eid Mubarak

Words that I learned today:

Sawm • Dawn • Ramadan • Iftar • Worship • Eid al-Fitr • Tarawih •

1. Color the correct box. When does Eid al-Fitr happen?

Before Ramadan	When Ramadan ends	In the middle of Ramadan

2. Color the correct box. What is the meaning of Fasting?

Not eating or drinking	Drinking water	Eating dates

3. Color the correct box. Muslims have a full-month of Sawm in the month of:

Muharram	Ramadan	Rajab

4. What is the name of the meal when you break the fast?

_____

5. Color this banner for Eid.

6. Match the words by drawing a line.

Eid al-Fitr   the month of fasting

Ramadan   fasting

Iftar   a day of happiness

Sawm   a breakfast at sunset

7. Circle the things we do on the day of Eid al-Fitr. Cross out the things we do not do on that day.

Fast.

Celebrate.

Have fun with family and friends.

Share food and money with the poor.

Zakah: *The Fourth Pillar*

Assalamu alaikum. Welcome to the class. Let us start by coloring Khalid who is helping in a charity.

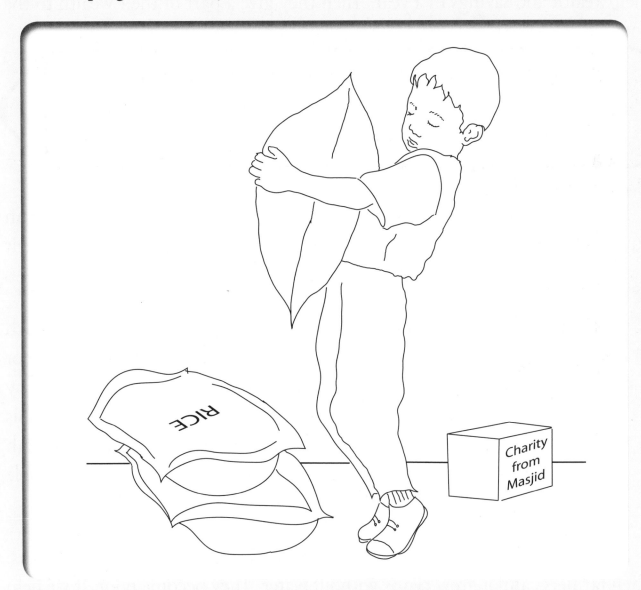

Zakah is the fourth pillar of Islam. The word Zakah means to clean or to purify. People pay zakah to purify their wealth. A simple meaning of zakah is **charity**. Charity is when you give something to help a needy person. We may give money, food or clothes to someone who does not have enough. We should help people who are needy.

Making salah and fasting are two important duties for all Muslims. The rich and the poor must make salah and fast. Zakah is also an important duty, but only for those Muslims who have enough money to pay it. People calculate their wealth and savings in a year. Then they give a part of their wealth to the poor.

Zakah means: to earn / to purify / to save

Zakah is given to a rich person.   True / False

The needy people can do many things with the help of Zakah. They can buy food, clothing and medicine. Zakah helps the needy people remove their problems.

People who are rich now, may not remain rich all the time. Sometimes people lose their money or their house. Sometimes a fire or flood may **destroy** a house or a shop. Sometimes a person may lose his job. When people are faced with a problem, Zakah can help them. If we give charity, then these people can build their homes or start a new business.

Sometimes, it does not rain for many months. Then farmers cannot grow **crops** without water. They become poor. If we help them, they can get new seeds for the next season.

Zakah helps to build a good **society**. A society is a group of people who live and work together. Not everyone in a society is rich. Some are poor. The rich have a duty to help the poor. Giving zakah reminds us that we live with other people. A good Muslim does not want anyone else to suffer. A rich person cannot give zakah to another rich person. A poor person need not give zakah because he does not have enough.

We can easily give money to others if we do not **waste**. We should never waste money. If we do not waste, then we will still have enough for ourselves, and we can give the saved money to the needy.

We should try to give zakah during Ramadan and other times. We should help our needy relatives, neighbors, and even people that we do not know. The Qur'an tells us who may get zakah and who may not.

Write Yes or No.

Can you give zakah to help someone buy a sports car. _____

Zakah is the 5th pillar of Islam. _____

Zakah should be paid by both rich and poor. _____

Words that I learned today:

Zakah • Charity • Destroy • Crops • Society • Waste •

1. How can zakah help the needy?

_____

_____

_____

2. Name four ways people may help the needy.

a. _____

b. _____

c. _____

d. _____

3. Fill in the blanks using the words given in the box.

fourth   Charity   society   waste

_____ is when you give something to help another person.

Zakah is the _____ pillar of Islam.

If we _____ our money, we cannot help others.

Zakah helps people build a good _____.

4. Mark with a ☑ if the person needs zakah. Mark with an ☒ if this person should not get zakah.

A man who owns an expensive car. ☐

A man who has no job and his family is hungry. ☐

An orphan who needs food and books. ☐

A family whose home is lost in an earthquake. ☐

A woman who lives in a mansion. ☐

A man who lost his shop in a flood. ☐

Hajj: *The Fifth Pillar*

Assalamu alaikum. Welcome to the class. Can you trace the path to the Ka'bah?

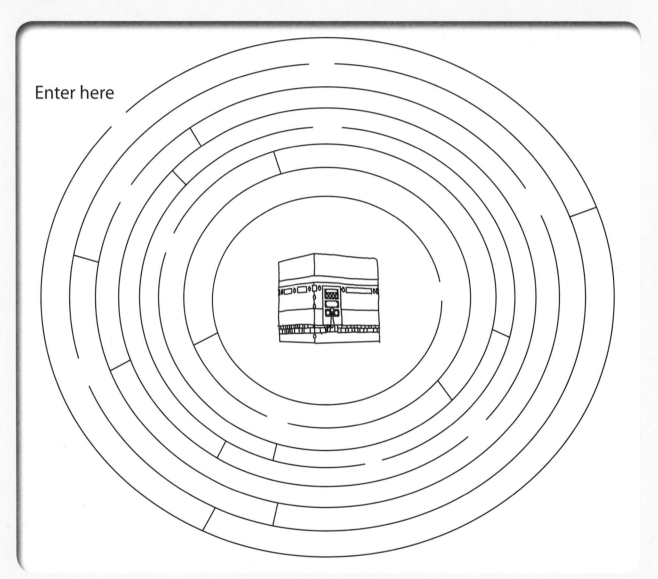

Enter here

Hajj is the fifth pillar of Islam. Hajj is a **pilgrimage**. Pilgrimage means a journey to a holy place. People who go for pilgrimage are **pilgrims**.

For Hajj, Muslims go to Makkah. Now Makkah is a large city. Thousands of years ago, it was not even a village. There were no trees or gardens. It was a rocky place, and it was very difficult to find any water to drink. Nobody lived in Makkah at that time.

During Hajj, we remember Prophet **Ibrahim** (A), who lived thousands of years ago. A long time ago, Ibrahim (A) brought his wife **Hajar** and his baby son **Ismail** **(A)** to Makkah. Baby Ismail (A) became very thirsty, and Hajar searched for water everywhere. She ran several times between two small hills **Safa** and **Marwah** looking for water. She and her baby became more tired and thirsty. At that time, Allah (swt) gave them a small spring of fresh water gushing out of the rocks. This spring is called **Zamzam**.

When Ismail (A) grew up, he and his father Ibrahim (A) built the Ka'bah once again. It is a simple house. Everyday, we make our salah facing the Ka'bah.

Mother Hajar had a son named _____

The spring in Makkah is known as _____

Hajj is held once every year. Muslims from all over the world come to Makkah for Hajj. They come by airplanes, ships, buses and cars.

During Hajj, all the men wear two pieces of white cloth called **Ihram**. All men look alike in the similar simple clothes. Women wear regular simple clothes.

When pilgrims reach Makkah, they walk around the Ka'bah seven times. This walking is called **Tawaf**. To remember mother Hajar, all the pilgrims walk seven times between Safa and Marwah.

Then all the pilgrims go to a place called **Mina**. This place has thousands of tents. The pilgrims go to a place called **Arafat**, and spend time in praying. They also spend a night under the sky.

There are three large walls in Mina. People throw small stones at these walls. This throwing reminds them to chase Shaitan away from their lives. The pilgrims then **sacrifice** an animal. If we cannot go for Hajj, we still sacrifice an animal on that day. The day people sacrifice an animal is the day of **Eid al-Adha**.

A Muslim, who has good health and enough money, should go for Hajj at least once in his or her life.

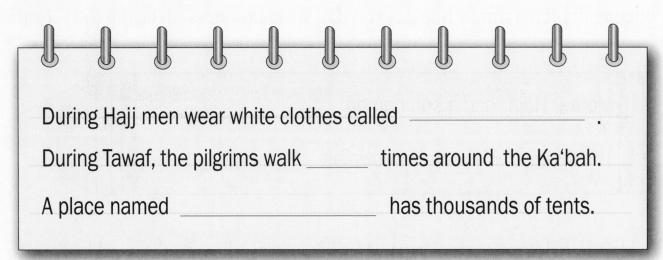

During Hajj men wear white clothes called ——————————— .

During Tawaf, the pilgrims walk _____ times around the Ka'bah.

A place named _____ has thousands of tents.

Words that I learned today:

Pilgrimage • Pilgrim • Ibrahim • Hajar • Ismail • Safa • Marwah • Zamzam • Ihram • Tawaf • Mina • Arafat • Sacrifice • Eid al-Adha •

1. What happened when baby Ismail (A) was thirsty?

_____

_____

_____

2. Find the following words in the puzzle.

> PILGRIM   IHRAM   TAWAF   MINA
>
> ARAFAT   ZAMZAM   SAFA

S	T	Z	A	M	Z	A	M
P	I	L	G	R	I	M	T
S	H	O	L	A	M	I	H
A	R	C	B	N	U	N	B
F	A	A	R	A	F	A	T
A	M	Y	T	A	W	A	F

3. Draw lines to connect the sentences together.

On Eid-al Adha   walking around the Ka'bah.

Ihram is two   there are many tents.

In Mina   pieces of white cloth.

Tawaf is   we sacrifice an animal.

4. Write YES if the sentence is correct, and write NO if it is not correct.

All the men wear two pieces of white cloth called Tawaf.   _____

Pilgrims throw small stones at large walls in Mina.   _____

We should sacrifice an animal on the day of Eid al-Fitr.   _____

Hajar found fresh water from a spring named Zamzam.   _____

5. extra**credit.** Ask your parents to help you find surah number 22 in the Qur'an. Then write down the name of the surah.

_____

Wudu: *Keep Our Bodies Clean*

Assalamu alaikum. Welcome to the class. Can you please color this boy who is making wudu?

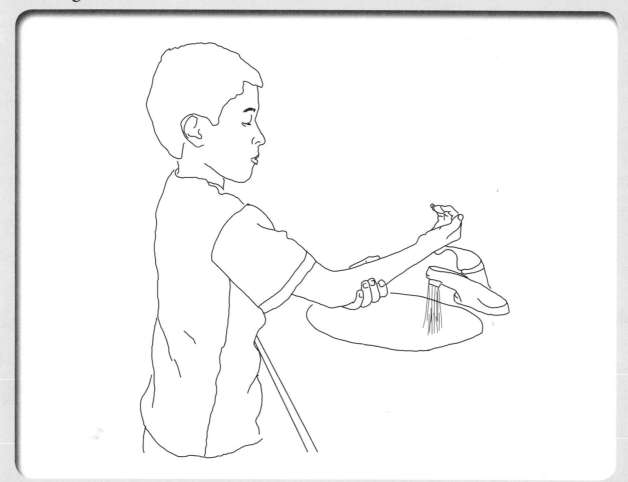

Before we can make salah, we have to make **wudu**. By making wudu we prepare our bodies and minds for salah. Wudu is about washing some parts of our bodies.

Wudu has several steps. We learn these steps from the Qur'an and from the teachings of Rasulullah (S).

Start with the name of Allah (swt) by saying Bismillahi-r Rahmani-r Rahim. Make an intention to make wudu silently.

1. We wash the right hand three times, and then we wash the left hand three times. In this step we wash up to the wrist of each hand.

2. We wash the inside of our mouths. We do it three times.

3. Then we **sniff** water inside our noses. We do it three times.

4. Then we wash our faces. Take water in both hands and wash the face from hairline to chin and from ear to ear. We do it three times.

5. Then we wash our right arms three times to the elbow. Then we wash the left arm three times to the elbow.

6. We then wipe our heads with our wet **palms**.

7. We clean our ear holes with a finger, and clean the back side of the ears.

8. With the back of our hand we wipe over the back of the neck once.

9. Then we wash our right foot three times to the ankle. Then we wash the left foot three times to the ankle.

Now we are ready to make salah. If you use the "bathroom", then you have to do wudu all over again before you can do a salah.

Words that I learned today:

Wudu • Sniff • Palms •

1. Fill in the blanks using the words from the box.

salah   hands   head   left

First we wash our right _____, then we wash our _____ hand.

We have to make wudu before we make _____.

The sixth step of wudu is to wipe your _____.

2. Circle the sentences that are correct, and cross out the sentences that are not correct.

When making wudu, we have to wash our entire body.

When making wudu, we have to wash our hair.

We can make salah without wudu.

When making wudu, we have to wash our arms.

3. Write any four parts of the body that should be **washed** in wudu. One is already filled for you.

a._____Hands_____   b. _____

c. _____   d. _____

4. You will need to practice making wudu at home everyday to become perfect. For this whole week, please mark the times that you practiced making wudu. If you think your wudu was not perfect, mark it with a red ☑, and if you think it was perfect, mark it with a green ☑.

	Fajr	Dhuhr	Asr	Maghrib	'Isha
Monday					
Tuesday					
Wednesday					
Thursday					
Friday					
Saturday					
Sunday					

Four Khalifas

Assalamu alaikum. Welcome to the class. Let us start by coloring the ovals that have the names of the first four khalifas.

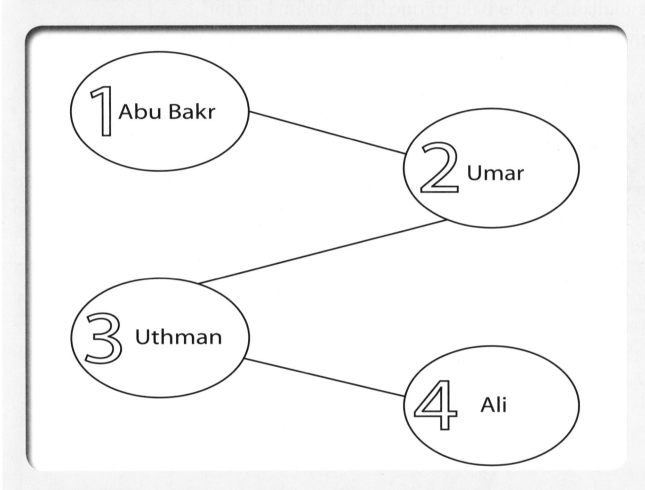

When Prophet Muhammad (S) was alive, he decided the rules of the country. People came to him with all major problems. He made sure that the country had a good system. Prophet Muhammad (S) was the leader of the Muslims.

After he passed away, several men became the leaders of the Muslims. They were not kings. They too made sure that the country was run by a good system. They were the **khalifas**. The first four were the best khalifas. They are called the **Rightly Guided Khalifas**.

Abu Bakr (r) was a close friend of Rasulullah (S). He was the first man to accept Islam. When Rasulullah (S) moved to Madinah, Abu Bakr (r) went with him. After Rasulullah (S) passed away, Abu Bakr (r) became the first khalifa. He was a kind and good leader. One of Abu Bakr's daughters was **Aishah (r)**. She was a wife of Rasulullah (S). Abu Bakr (r) ruled the Muslim land for only two years. In this short time, he handled many problems in the country.

When Abu Bakr passed away, **Umar (r)** became the second khalifa. When he was a young man, he did not like the Muslims or Prophet Muhammad (S). Then his mind changed and he became a Muslim. He became a good friend of Rasulullah (S). He helped Rasulullah (S) in many ways. Rasulullah (S) married one of Umar's daughters. Umar (r) was a good, brave and strict leader. He made a large Islamic country. He made many changes in order to make the Islamic land a better place to live. He took care of the people under his rule. He ruled for ten years.

For how many years did Abu Bakr (r) rule?

For how many years did Umar (r) rule?

Whose daughter was Aishah (r)?

The third khalifa was **Uthman (r)**. He was born in to a rich family. When he became Muslim, many rich people started to become Muslim. He was a

khalifa for twelve years. During his rule, the Islamic land became very large. He made many copies of the Qur'an and sent them all over the country.

The fourth khalifa was **Ali (r)**. He was the son-in-law of Rasulullah (S). When Ali (r) was a little boy, he became a Muslim. He was a strong fighter. He helped the Muslims win many

battles. He was a khalifa for five years. He wrote many important books in Arabic.

After Ali (r) passed away, several other rulers became khalifas. These khalifas ruled for hundreds of years. They were not known as the Rightly Guided Khalifas.

	Which Khalifa ruled for the longest period?
	Which Khalifa ruled for the shortest period?
	How long did 'Ali (r) rule as Khalifa?

Words that I learned today:

Khalifa • Abu Bakr • Aishah • Umar • Uthman • Ali • Rightly Guided Khalifa •

homework weekend 13

1. Write the names of the first four Khalifas.

a. ______________________

b. ______________________

c. ______________________

d. ______________________

2. Find the following words in the puzzle.

KHALIFA ABU BAKR UMAR UTHMAN
ALI AISHAH ISLAM

A	T	N	O	U	A	W	A
B	H	C	E	T	S	I	I
U	A	L	I	H	H	A	S
B	F	N	V	M	G	K	H
A	N	U	M	A	R	Q	A
K	C	X	N	N	K	J	H
R	G	I	S	L	A	M	K
I	K	H	A	L	I	F	A

3. What happened to the Islamic land when Uthman was the khalifa?

_____

_____

_____

4. Fill in the blanks using the words from the box.

| Khalifas   Abu Bakr   Umar   Uthman   Ali |

_____ (r) ruled for 10 years.

_____ (r) wrote many important books.

There were many _____, but the first four were the Rightly Guided Khalifas.

_____ (r) made many copies of the Qur'an and sent them all over the country.

_____ (r) was the first man to accept Islam and the first khalifa.

Ibrahim (A): *A Friend of Allah*

Assalamu alaikum. Welcome to the class. Let us color this sunrise. Ibrahim (A) knew that only Allah (swt) could make the sun rise from the east.

Several thousand years ago, there was a prophet whose name was **Ibrahim** (A). He was born in Iraq. As with other prophets, he too was a brave and honest prophet. He told his people to worship only Allah (swt), but the people were always angry at him. These people thought there were many gods, and they made pictures of their gods and made **idols**. They forgot about Allah (swt).

One day, Ibrahim (A) went to a temple alone and broke many idols. He wanted people to understand that idols were not god. Later, the people saw that the idols were in pieces. All these days the people believed that their idols had power. Now the people saw that the idols could not even save themselves. The idols could not even tell who broke them. Most of the people were angry, but a few understood. These few people were **ashamed** for worshipping idols. They understood that idols cannot be gods. The angry people wanted to burn Ibrahim (A), but Allah (swt) saved him.

One day Ibrahim (A) went to see a king. The king thought he was a very powerful god. Ibrahim (A) told him that if he was a god he should make the sun rise from the west. The king could not do that. He learned that he was not the God.

What did Ibrahim (A) do in the temple?

Where was Ibrahim (A) born?

Can a king make the sun rise from the west?

From Iraq Ibrahim (A) went to live in Egypt. He had two sons, **Ismail** (A) and **Ishaq** (A). When both the sons grew up, they too became prophets of Allah (swt). They all followed the religion of Islam.

Ibrahim (A) lived in Makkah for some time. Makkah had a house called the Ka'bah, but it was broken down. Ibrahim (A) and Ismail (A) put the stones together to build the Ka'bah all over again. They prayed that everyone should worship to Allah (swt) only. Allah (swt) listened to their prayer. Allah (swt) later made the Ka'bah our **Qiblah**. The word Qiblah means we make our salah facing the Ka'bah in Makkah. Allah (swt) loved Ibrahim (A) very much. Ibrahim (A) was a friend of Allah (swt).

Name three places where Ibrahim (A) lived. _____

_____

What is our Qiblah? _____

You know that Shaitan is bad, and he wants us to do bad things. One day, Shaitan came up to Ibrahim (A) and Ismail (A). Shaitan told them, "Do not listen to Allah!" Do you know what happened? Ibrahim (A) picked up some rocks, and threw these at Shaitan! He did this to chase away Shaitan.

If you go for Hajj, you will also throw stones at Shaitan to chase him away from your life. We do not want Shaitan to be our friend.

Words that I learned today:

Ibrahim (A) • Idols • Ashamed • Ismail (A) • Ishaq (A) •
Qiblah •

1. What are the two ways Ibrahim (A) proved that Allah was the only God?

_____

_____

_____

_____

_____

2. Write YES if the sentence is correct, and write NO if it is not correct.

Ibrahim (A) had two sons who grew up to be prophets. _____

Ibrahim (A) and Ismail (A) built the Ka'bah all over again. _____

Shaitan went up to Ibrahim (A) and Ismail (A) and asked them to listen to Allah (swt). _____

Allah (swt) made the Ka'bah the Qiblah because He listened the prayer of Ibrahim (A). _____

3. extra**credit.** Ask your parents to help you find surah number 14 in the Qur'an. Then write down the name of the surah.

_____

4. Solve this crossword puzzle.

Across:

1. The place where Ibrahim (A) was born.

3. The religion that Ibrahim (A) followed.

4. This prophet was a friend of Allah (swt).

6. People of Ibrahim (A) did not believe in Him.

Down:

2. Allah made the Ka'bah our _____

4. Ibrahim (A) broke some of them.

5. This prophet helped his father rebuild the Ka'bah.

Yaqub (A) and Yusuf (A)

Assalamu alaikum. Welcome to the class. Let us start by coloring this deep well in an open field.

Last week, we learned that Ibrahim (A) had two sons, Ismail (A) and Ishaq (A). Both the sons were prophets of Allah (swt). When Ishaq (A) grew up, he had a son named **Yaqub** (A). He was also a prophet of Allah (swt). Yaqub (A) is a grandson of Ibrahim (A).

When Yaqub (A) grew up, he started a family. He had twelve sons. One of his sons was **Yusuf** (A). He too was a prophet of Allah (swt). Yusuf (A) was a great-grandson of Ibrahim (A), and a grandson of Ishaq (A).

Yaqub (A) loved his young son Yusuf (A) very much. Some brothers did not like that their father loved Yusuf (A). These brothers were bad. One day, they took little Yusuf (A) to a playground for a game. The playground had a **deep well**. A well is a deep hole in the ground where you can get water. Yusuf (A)'s brothers pushed him into the well. Little Yusuf (A) could not climb out of the well. The bad brothers told their father that a **wolf** ate Yusuf (A) up. Yaqub (A) did not believe his sons.

Who was the grandfather of Yusuf (A)? _____

The bad brothers left Yusuf (A) in a: _____

Later, some people came to get water from the well. They picked up Yusuf (A). They then sold him to a rich family in **Egypt**. Yusuf (A) grew up there. He became a wise man. He could tell the meanings of dreams!

One day, the king heard that Yusuf (A) knew many things. The king asked Yusuf (A) to work for the kingdom. Yusuf (A) had a big job. He made sure that the kingdom had lots of food for years to come.

After some years, dry seasons started. There was no rain. People could not grow crops. They had no food. Yusuf (A) had stored extra food for the people. Many people came to Yusuf (A) to get food for their families. The bad brothers also came to get some food. They did not know that their brother Yusuf (A) was now giving out food. They believed Yusuf (A) died long back in the well. Yusuf (A) did not tell them who he was. He asked them to bring the youngest brother next time. When the youngest brother came to Egypt, he was blamed for stealing. Yusuf (A) saved him because he did not steal. Then Yusuf (A) told his brothers who he was. His brothers were sorry for what they did to Yusuf (A) long ago.

Yusuf (A) asked his brothers to bring their father to Egypt. He was very happy to see his father after many years. Allah (swt) is very kind. He **united** a father and his good son.

Yusuf (A) was brought to a family in: _____

Yusuf (A) knew the meanings of: _____

The brothers came to Egypt to get: _____

Words that I learned today:

Yaqub (A) • Yusuf (A) • Deep well • Wolf • Egypt • United •

1. Complete the family tree of prophet Yusuf (A). One box has already been filled for you.

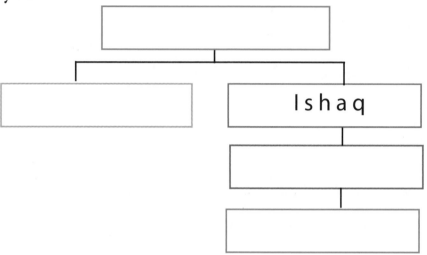

2. Find the words in the word search.

YAQUB   YUSUF   WOLF   COURT   UNITED   WELL   FOOD

```
L  Y  A  Q  U  B  F  K
U  F  R  T  E  H  O  W
Y  W  E  B  A  R  O  E
C  O  U  R  T  S  D  L
M  L  Y  U  S  U  F  L
P  F  U  N  I  T  E  D
```

3. What did Yusuf (A)'s brothers do to him when he was a child?

_____

_____

_____ .

4. Write YES if the sentence is correct. Write NO if it is not correct.

Yusuf (A)'s brothers told Yaqub (A) that a bear ate him.   _____

Yusuf (A) grew up with a rich family after he got out of the well.   _____

Yusuf (A)'s brothers asked him for food.   _____

Yusuf (A) and Yaqub (A) were united after many years.   _____

5. extra**credit.** Ask your parents to help you find surah 12 in the Qur'an. Then write down the name of the surah.

_____

Musa (A) and Harun (A)

Assalamu alaikum. Welcome to the class. Let us color this basket floating in the water.

Once upon a time, there was a prophet in **Egypt**. His name was **Musa** (A). Musa (A) had a brother named **Harun** (A). He was also a prophet. They were from a poor family.

In those days, the ruler of Egypt was **Pharaoh**. He was not a good ruler. He was mean to the poor people. He did not believe in Allah (swt). He thought he was a god. He was afraid that a little baby boy from among the poor families would one day destroy him. He did not know which baby boy it would be. So, he ordered to kill all baby boys. The army began to kill many baby boys.

Musa (A) was a little baby at that time. His mother became worried. "What will happen to my Musa?" she thought. Allah (swt) told her to place baby Musa (A) in a basket and let him float down the river. She believed Allah (swt) would help Musa (A). The basket slowly floated, and it reached Pharaoh's palace! The queen was surprised and happy to see a baby boy inside the basket. She adopted the boy as her son. Allah (swt) saved Musa (A). Pharaoh could not kill him.

Pharaoh ordered to kill all baby boys and girls.   Yes / No

Baby Musa (A) was placed in a _____ in a river.

Who picked up baby Musa (A) from the river? _____

When Musa (A) grew up, Allah (swt) made him a prophet. Allah (swt) asked him to help the poor people. Both Musa (A) and Harun (A) went to Pharaoh to tell him about Allah (swt). They told Pharaoh not to torture the poor people.

Pharaoh asked Musa (A) to show him a sign from Allah (swt). Musa (A) 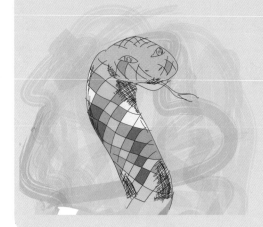 threw his stick to the ground and it became a snake. Pharaoh thought it was **magic**. He then called some **magicians** to show better magic. They brought sticks and ropes, which also became snakes. Musa (A) threw his stick again. It became a snake, and ate up the other snakes. The magicians became sure that Musa (A) was a prophet of Allah (swt) and they became Muslims.

One day, Allah (swt) asked Musa (A) to take the poor people away from Pharaoh. Musa (A) took them to a far away land. Then he went to a hill to learn more from Allah (swt). While Musa (A) was gone, these people forgot about Allah (swt). They made a cow out of gold and started to worship it. Harun (A) told them not to worship anything but Allah (swt). But they became angry with him. "The cow is our god," they said.

When Musa (A) came back from the hill, he became angry at the people. He told them to worship only Allah (swt). The people were sorry for their actions. They faced bad times for worshipping the cow.

Pharaoh asked Musa (A) to show _____ of Allah (swt).

Musa's (A) snake ate up the magician's _____

People built a cow made of _____ to worship as their god.

Words that I learned today:

Egypt • Musa • Harun • Pharaoh • Magic • Magicians •

1. Musa (A) and Harun (A) were: (Color the correct box)

| Father and son | Two brothers | A king and a magician |

2. Musa (A) and Harun (A) lived in: (Color the correct oval)

Iraq   Morocco   Egypt

3. When Musa (A) threw down his stick, it became a: (Color the correct box)

| Bird | Snake | Camel |

4. The people of Musa (A) had worshipped a: (Color the correct oval)

Monkey   Bear   Cow

5. Fill in the blanks using the words from the box:

| queen | hill | gold | basket |

The mother put baby Musa (A) in a _____.

At the palace the _____ found a baby from the river.

When the people made a cow, Musa (A) was on a _____.

The people worshipped a cow made of _____.

6. Mark with a ☑ if it is correct. Mark with an ☒ if it is wrong.

Even if a king wants to harm someone, Allah (swt) can save him. ☐

Worshipping a cow is a bad idea. ☐

The basket carrying Musa (A) reached Makkah. ☐

Harun (A) and the king made a golden cow. ☐

The magician's snake ate the stick of Musa (A). ☐

7. **extracredit.** Is it possible that Musa (A) and Harun (A) came after Muhammad (S)? Write your answer based on what you learned in the weekend4 lesson of this book. (Hint: think of the Last Prophet).

_____

Yunus (A)

Assalamu alaikum. Welcome to the class. Let us start by coloring this gourd plant and its big leaves.

A long time ago, there was a land where many bad people lived. They would lie, steal, and hurt other people. They did not believe in Allah (swt). To guide them, Allah (swt) sent a prophet. His name was **Yunus** (A).

Yunus (A) told his people to believe in Allah (swt). He tried very hard, but nobody would listen to him. He tried again. Still nobody would listen to him.

It seemed that his people would never become good. Yunus (A) became very upset with them.

Yunus (A) did not want to talk to his people any more. He left his land and got onto a ship. He wanted to go far away.

As the ship went to the sea, the weather became bad. Big waves came. It rained hard. The waves tossed and bounced the ship. The **sailors** became afraid. "Will the ship sink?" the sailors thought.

The sailors thought that maybe someone on the ship brought bad luck. They thought that if the person was removed from the ship, then the sea would be quiet. The sailors picked a name by doing a lottery. In the lottery they picked the name of Yunus (A)!

The sailors then threw Yunus (A) into the sea. Yunus (A) started to sink. But Allah (swt) helped him. Allah sent a big fish to help Yunus (A). The fish gulped him up. Yunus (A) entered the body of the fish. It was dark and quiet. He prayed to Allah (swt) to forgive him.

Yunus (A) left his people because they did not: _____

Yunus (A) got into a _____ to go away from his people.

Sailors picked Yunus (A)'s name by doing a _____

The fish swam with Yunus (A). It came close to a **shore** and left Yunus (A) on there. Yunus (A) was very tired. He had been in the rough sea, and then

inside the body of the fish. He was now on a lonely, very sunny and hot beach. He was looking for shade, but there was none. He was too weak to walk. So he slept on the burning hot sand. Then Allah (swt) helped him again. A **gourd** plant grew there and gave him shade with its big leaves.

When Yunus (A) became stronger, he went back to his town. He tried once again to tell the people about Allah (swt). This time most of the people listened to Yunus (A) and started believing in Allah (swt). Yunus (A) tried and Allah (swt) helped him to become successful.

The big fish left Yunus (A) on a: _____

A _____ plant grew and gave Yunus (A) shade.

When Yunus (A) returned, his people _____ to him.

Words that I learned today:

Yunus • Sailors • Shore • Gourd •

1. Mark with a ☑ if it is correct. Mark with an ☒ if it is wrong.

Yunus (A) left his town by bus. ☐

The sailors helped Yunus (A) when the weather was bad. ☐

The ship carrying Yunus (A) sailed in bad weather. ☐

The big fish brought Yunus (A) to shore. ☐

Allah (swt) can save you even if you are in a big storm. ☐

2. Fill in the blanks using the words from the box.

tired	sailors	prayed	fish	gourd

A _____ plant has big leaves.

On the shore, Yunus (A) was very _____.

Allah (swt) sent a big _____ to help Yunus (A) after her was thrown into the sea.

Yunus (A) _____ to Allah to forgive him.

The _____ decided to throw Yunus (A) into the sea.

3. From the life of Yunus (A), we learn many things. Write **Yes** if the sentence is correct. Write **No** if it is not the teaching.

Allah (swt) helps us only one time. _____

When we try, Allah (swt) helps us. _____

We should pray to only one Allah (swt). _____

If we cannot do our math problem, we should try again. _____

We should give up doing good work after doing it once. _____

4. Pictures A and B have six differences. Circle the differences.

A

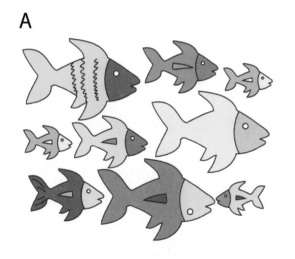

B

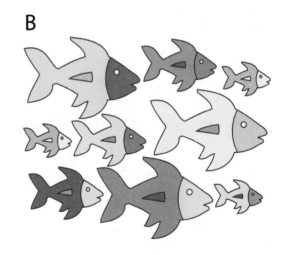

5. extra**credit.** Ask your parents to help you find surah number 10 in the Qur'an. Then write down the name of the surah.

_____

Angels: *Our Helpers*

Assalamu alaikum. Welcome to the class. Let us start by coloring this mountain, called **Jabal An-Nur**. Cave Hira is in this mountain. Angel Jibril brought the first verses of the Qur'an to Prophet Muhammad (S) in this cave.

As Muslims, we believe in angels. In Arabic, angels are called **malak**. Angels are created out of light, just as we are created out of clay. Allah (swt) created angels to do many duties. They never get tired of doing their duties. They always listen to Allah (swt). They never disobey Allah (swt) because they do not have a choice.

One of the main duties of angels is to praise Allah (swt). Another duty is to help people. Whenever we do a good thing, an angel writes it down. All

Muslims believe in **Angels**

our good work will help us go to Heaven. When we go to Heaven, the angels will welcome us. If we do a bad thing, angels write it down. We cannot hide any bad thing from Allah (swt). We should be careful, and not do bad things.

We do not see the angels, but they are always around us. When we do a good job, the angels help us. The angels always helped our Rasulullah (S), because he was the best man. Once a large number of bad people came to fight with our Prophet Muhammad (S) and the Muslims. At that time, Muslims were only a few in number. The enemies were strong. As the Muslims were good people, many angels came to help them. The enemies lost the battle. They had to run away.

Angels are created out of _____.

Angels never get _____ of doing their duty.

The main duty of angels is to _____ Allah (swt).

Angels write down our _____ and _____ works.

The angels do many jobs for Allah (swt). They always listen to His orders. Angel **Jibril** had the big job of bringing the Qur'an to our Rasulullah (S). One night, Muhammad (S) was inside a cave called **Hira**. At that time Angel Jibril brought him some verses of the Qur'an. Angel Jibril told Muhammad (S) that he was to be a prophet of Allah. For the next 23 years, angel Jibril continued to bring verses of the Qur'an to Rasulullah (S).

After creating the first man Adam (A), Allah (swt) asked the angels to **bow down** to man. All the angels bowed down. The angels agreed to help the people. The angels pray to Allah (swt) for us. They save us from bad things.

When we need help, we make **du'a** to Allah (swt). When Allah (swt) orders the angels, they help us do our job. They never say no to Allah (swt).

We know the names of some of the angels. They are:

JIBRIL   MIKAL   ISRAFIL   AZRAEL

MALIK   HARUT   MARUT

Angel **Mikal** brings rewards for us. Angel **Israfil** will blow a trumpet when the world will end. Angel **Azrael** takes our souls when we die. Angel **Malik** will bring the punishments in the Hell fire. We also know the names of two angels **Harut** and **Marut**.

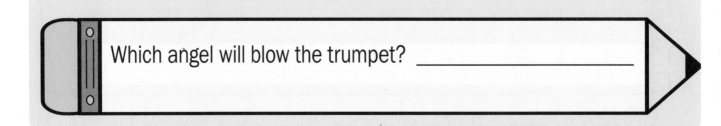

Which angel will blow the trumpet? _____

Words that I learned today:

Jabal An-Nur • Malak • Jibril • Hira • Bow down • Du'a • Mikal • Israfil • Azrael • Malik • Harut • Marut •

1. Write the names of six angels as given in the lesson.

    1._____

    2._____

    3._____

    4._____

    5._____

    6._____

2. In Arabic, angels are called: (Color the correct oval)

    Hira   Malak   Jabal

3. Angels are made out of: (Color the correct box)

    Clay   Skin   Light

4. The Qur'an started to come when Muhammad (S) was in: (Color the correct triangle)

△ Egypt   △ Cave Hira   △ Cave Harut

5. When we are in difficulty, angels help us.

Should we then pray to angels to help us?   Write **Yes** or **No**. _____

Whom should we pray to for help? _____

6. Draw lines to match the names of the angels with their jobs.

Jibril   Punishment in Hell

Israfil   Bring the Qur'an

Mikal   Blow the Trumpet

Malik   Brings rewards

7. Why do you think the angels helped the Muslims against the bad people?

_____

_____

Food That We May Eat

Assalamu alaikum. Today we will color this dinner plate. Allah (swt) has given us so much good food.

Allah (swt) has given us different kinds of food. All the foods are gifts from Allah (swt). He has also given us rules about eating our food.

Allah (swt) allows us to eat all good foods. These are **halal** food. There are other foods that Allah (swt) does not want us to eat. Such foods are called **haram**.

Before we eat any food we say, *Bismillahir Rahmanir Rahim*. We remember Allah (swt), and thank Him for His gifts to us.

Allah (swt) allows us to eat all kinds of fruits and vegetables. All fruits and vegetables are halal. Some meats are halal, some are haram. Halal meats are from good animals, such as cows, lambs and chickens. In order to make these halal, the meats of these animals are prepared in an **Islamic** way by remembering Allah (swt). The Islamic way of killing and preparing meat of an animal is called **Zabiha**. Fish are also halal to eat.

Food that we are allowed to eat are: halal / haram

A halal meat is prepared in an _____ way.

The meat of pig is haram. We do not eat any meat from pigs. Such meats may be called as **pork, ham, sausage** or **bacon**. As Muslims, we do not eat any of these meats. Before we eat any boxed or canned food, it is a good idea to check the list of **ingredients**. If we see any pork items, we should not eat it.

Allah (swt) wants us to eat only those foods that are healthy for us. We should not eat rotten food or any foods that are not good for us. We also should not waste food. It is not good to eat too much or too little.

We can eat the food made by the Christians and the Jews, if the food is halal. If we know that a food was offered to an idol or false god, then we cannot eat that food.

Some non-Muslim people drink **wine** or **beer**. These are called **alcohol**. A Muslim is not allowed to drink alcohol.

When we finish eating, we should thank Allah (swt) for His gifts to us. We should say "*Alhamdulillah.*"

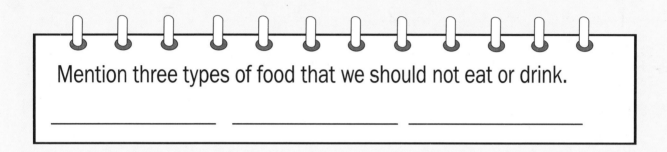

Mention three types of food that we should not eat or drink.

_____   _____   _____

Words that I learned today:

Halal • Haram • Islamic • Zabiha • Pork • Ham • Sausage • Bacon • Ingredients • Wine • Beer • Alcohol •

1. Write over the circles five kinds of food that we should not eat.

1.

2.

3.

4.

5.

2. What should we say before we eat anything?

_____

3. Let us write some antonyms (words that have opposite meanings). One is already done for you.

Good   Bad

Halal   _____

Hard   _____

Day   _____

Haram   _____

4. Zabiha is the proper way of: (Color the correct box)

| Washing a fish | Killing an animal for food | Making juice |

5. Before we buy canned or boxed food, we should look at the: (Color the correct oval)

(List of ingredients)   (Picture of animals)   (Color of the can or box)

6. We should read the list of ingredients to see if the food has: (Color the correct box)

| Hidden gifts | Haram items | Puzzles |

7. extra**credit.** We should not waste good <u>halal</u> food. You are somewhere, and someone gives you a sandwich. It has bacon! What should you do?

_____

_____

Truthfulness

Assalamu alaikum. Welcome to the class. Let us color Tahira who is doing her homework. She always does her homework on time.

Everyday, we should try to be **truthful**. This means that we should speak the truth and act in a correct manner. If we do not speak the truth, then we are lying. Allah (swt) does not love those people who lie. He loves those who speak the truth.

We can learn many good things from the life of our Prophet Muhammad (S). He always spoke the truth, even before he became a prophet. Because he was truthful, people loved him and trusted him. The people of Makkah used to call him **Al-Amin**, the **trustworthy**. All the prophets were also truthful people. In their lives they had many difficulties, but they never gave up truth.

A person who does not speak the truth forgets about Allah (swt). This person thinks nobody will know that he is lying. Allah (swt) always knows who is speaking the truth and who is not. We cannot hide anything from Him. If we do not speak the truth, many times our parents and teachers can find it out. It is never a good idea to tell lies.

On which day we should be truthful?   Friday / Everyday

Who was known as Al-Amin?

Sometimes it is OK to tell a lie to our parents and teachers.   Yes / No

If we do good things, then we can always speak the truth. People lie when they do bad things. If you do your homework on time, then you do not have to make up a story. Making up a story is lying. In the picture, Tahira is doing her homework on time so that she does not have to make up a story.

We get many rewards for being truthful. Many verses of the Qur'an say that Allah (swt) will bless the truthful people. Such people will be in the Paradise.

Many hadith of the Prophet (S) remind us to be truthful. One hadith teaches us that if we are truthful, then we can go to Heaven.

Your parents will love you more if you speak the truth. Your teacher and friends will like you if you always speak the truth.

Allah (swt) tells us to speak the truth. Shaitan tells us to lie. We should not listen to Shaitan. He is not our friend. Shaitan wants us to get into **trouble**. When we lie, we get into trouble. Shaitan becomes happy. We do not want to make Shaitan happy.

If we do something bad, we should not try to cover it up with lies. We should say sorry to Allah (swt). Saying sorry to Allah (swt) means that we make **tawbah**. Allah (swt) is very kind, and forgives us when we make tawbah.

How many prophets were truthful? _____

Truthful people will go to _____

What does Shaitan tell us to do? _____

Words that I learned today:
Truthful • Al-Amin • Trustworthy • Trouble • Tawbah •

1. What is the meaning of being truthful? (Hint: The answer is in the first paragraph of the lesson).

_____

_____

2. Write a few rewards we get for being truthful.

a. _____

b. _____

c. _____

3. Who tells us to speak the Truth?

_____

4. Who tells us to lie?

_____

5. Where will the truthful people be after they die?

_____

6. Arrange these jumbled letters into meaningful words.

_ _ _ T _

_ _ A _ _ _ _

R _ _ _ _ _ _

Kindness

Assalamu alaikum. Welcome to the class. Let us color this picture of little Asma. She is a kind girl who loves to feed hungry birds.

You show **kindness** when you help or support someone. Kindness is being nice to others. We are kind when we make things easy for others.

We can be kind to people who are younger than us, and also to those who are older than us. We can show kindness in many ways. When we smile at someone, we are being kind to him. When we **praise** someone for good work, we are being kind to him. If we give a hug, we are being kind. When we do not hurt others feelings, we are being kind to them. When we say *salam* to someone, we are being kind. Have you been kind to someone today?

A good Muslim is kind to people, animals and plants. We should not hurt any animal for fun. We should not pluck plants or flowers just for fun.

When Prophet Muhammad (S) and the Muslims were in Madinah, the **idol worshippers** fought against them. When the Prophet (S) came back to Makkah as a winner, he was very kind. He did not punish the idol worshippers, but he forgave them. This was a great act of kindness. The idol-worshippers were won over by his kindness. They became Muslim.

The Qur'an has a surah called *Al-Ma'un* or **Acts of Kindness**. In this surah, Allah (swt) tells us to be kind. Allah (swt) tells us that it is not good to make salah but not show kindness to others.

A good Muslim is kind to others. Muslims should help others who are in difficulty. You can help others by giving zakah. You can also help your mother by helping her at home. You can be kind to others by saying to them "*Jazakallah khair*", or "May Allah bless you", or "May Allah protect you." When someone does a good job, say "*Masha-Allah*." Saying good words with a smile is being kind.

> Which surah is known as *Act of Kindness*? _____
>
> What did Prophet Muhammad (S) do to the idol worshipper after returning to Makkah? _____
>
> We should be kind to people, animals and plants.   True / False

Islam teaches us to be kind to our parents. When they become old, we should still treat them well and be kind to them. We should talk to them politely. Our Prophet (S) said that those who are kind to others, Allah (swt) is kind to them. Our Prophet (S) also said that Allah loves the kind people.

If you are kind to someone, it does not mean you are weak. You can be kind to someone only if you are strong. A **hero** is someone who is kind, not someone who is mean.

Everyday we get many chances to be kind. Can you think of new ways to be kind to your friend, brother, sister, mother or father?

Write below three things you can do to show kindness to others.

a) _____

b) _____

c) _____

Words that I learned today:

Kindness • Praise • Idol worshippers • Al-Ma'un • Jazakallah khair • Masha-Allah • Hero •

1. Color all the ovals that show the correct meanings of kindness:

   Help or support someone   Not being mean to others

   Give someone a hard time   Make things easy for others

2. Write three different ways that you can be kind to your mother or father.

   _____

   _____

   _____

3. Write two different ways that you can be kind to your friend.

   _____

   _____

4. Write **T** if the sentence is true, write **F** if it is false.

   We have to be kind only to our parents, not to others.   _____

   We have to be kind only to people, not to animals.   _____

   Allah is kind to those people who are kind to others.   _____

5. Mark with a ☑ if it is an act of kindness. Mark with an ☒ if it is rude or mean.

Feeding hungry birds or cats. ☐

Smiling at your friends. ☐

Pushing your friend's books on to the floor. ☐

Watering the plants in your garden. ☐

Pushing others while standing in the lunch line. ☐

6. extra**credit.** Ask your parent to find Surah Al-Ma'un in the Qur'an for you. It is surah 107. Count the number of ayat or verses in this surah. How many verses are in Surah Al- Ma'un?

_____

Respect

Assalamu alaikum. Welcome to the class. Let us color these two boys who are **greeting** each other with respect.

Respect is to treat someone or something with honor. We should treat others the way we want them to treat us. This is respect. Do you want someone to be mean to you? If not, then we should not be mean to others. We should show respect to people who are older and younger than us.

Our parents love us very much and we love our parents. Allah (swt) tells us to respect our parents. A good Muslim never treats the parents in a bad way. We should never say any bad words to them.

Our dear prophet Muhammad (S) is the last prophet and the prophet for the whole world. We love him and respect him. When we say his name, we add **Sallahu Alaihi Wa Sallam** to show respect. Allah (swt) had sent some prophets who came before Muhammad (S). We must respect all the prophets in the same way. We should say **Alaihi Sallam** after their name.

After Allah's name we say **Subhan-hu wa Ta'ala** to show respect. The Qur'an is the Book of Allah (swt). We touch it with clean hands, and we keep it clean. We respect the Qur'an and take care of it. We read the Qur'an with respect.

After Allah's name we say:

After Prophet Muhammad's name we say:

After past prophet's name we say:

As Muslims, we should not make fun of other religions, even though Islam is the only religion of Allah (swt). Even today, some people worship pictures and idols and think these are their gods. We should not make fun of them.

We respect the **property** of others. Property could be toys, books, bikes, cars or even a house. We cannot take other people's property without asking them. We should not harm other people's property.

We show respect to others by being nice to them. If someone is nice to us, we should be nicer. Allah (swt) teaches us not to laugh at others because they may be better than us. The Qur'an teaches us not to **tease** others. It is not good to call others names.

The Qur'an teaches us to respect the **privacy** of other people. Privacy is what you do not want others to see or know. We should not try to find out what they are doing in their own time and place. The Qur'an teaches us to enter people's houses after getting permission. This is to show respect for them. When someone is talking, we should listen carefully. Only when they are done speaking, should we speak.

We should show respect to everything around us. This makes the world a better place.

We need not show respect to other religions.   True / False

We need not show respect to poor people.   True / False

We touch the Qur'an with _____ to show respect.

Words that I learned today:

Greeting • Respect • Property • Tease • Privacy •

1. What is respect? (Hint: The answer is in the first paragraph of the lesson).

_____

_____

2. How should a good Muslim treat his or her mother?

_____

_____

3. We must show respect to: (Color the correct box)

| All the prophets | Muhammad (S) only | None of the prophets |

4. We must show respect to: (Color the correct box)

| Islam only | All the religions | None of the religions |

5. If someone says "Assalamu alaikum" what should we say in return?

_____

6. Circle all the correct choices. As a good Muslim child I show respect to:

Teacher	Doctor	Father	Mother
Principal	Nurse	Muadhdhin	Student
Firefighter	Plumber	Salesman	Lawyer
Senator	Imam	Pilot	Waiter

7. Why should we not laugh at others?

_____

_____

Responsibility

Assalamu alaikum. Welcome to the class. Let us color this girl who is a safe bicycle rider. She is responsible, wears a helmet and rides carefully.

Responsibility is a big word. It means something that is a duty or job.

If your teacher tells you to do your homework, then you are responsible for doing it on time. Your homework is your duty, so you are responsible for it.

We are responsible for something that we own or **control**. As a kid, you are not responsible for driving a car. If you have a bike, then you are responsible for riding it safely. If you have a pet, then you have to feed and take care of it. As you grow up, your responsibilities will **increase**.

Responsibility also means to think and use our brains, and to act in a good way. If you turn off a running water **faucet**, you acted responsibly. If somebody tells you to do a bad thing, you should think twice. If you do not do the bad thing, you have acted responsibly.

A good Muslim is a responsible person. A good Muslim finishes his or her work on time. Allah (swt) has given us salah at fixed times. We can learn to be responsible by praying salah on time. A responsible child uses his or her time in a good way.

We are responsible if we can control what we do. If we talk or scream during our classes, then we are not responsible.

While in a masjid, we can practice to be responsible. We learn to sit quietly while the Imam is talking. During Ramadan, we learn to be responsible. We learn to control our hunger. We learn how not to become angry at others.

Draw and color the other half of the masjid

We are responsible for keeping our rooms clean. We should keep our desk clean. We should keep our books in the right places. Once we are done playing, we should put the toys away in their right places. These are our responsibilities. Helping our parents with different **chores** teaches us responsibility.

We should not make **excuses** if we do not finish a job. We are responsible to do our own jobs. If we leave a job halfway done, then we did not show responsibility. When our parents give us a task, we should finish it. We should not wait to be reminded again and again.

To put blame on others is not good. If we do something wrong, then we should own the blame. To blame others means to walk away from responsibility. Then we are not being honest or truthful.

Allah (swt) tells us that we are responsible for our own work. We are responsible for our own salah and our own fasting. Nobody else can do our salah or fasting for us.

We cannot learn responsibility in a day. If we keep trying everyday, we will become responsible.

Give three examples when you showed responsibility.

a.

b.

c.

Words that I learned today:

Responsibility • Control • Increase • Faucet • Chores • Excuses •

1. What is responsibility? (Hint: The answer is in the first paragraph of the lesson).

_____

_____

2. Write four things that you are responsible for. (Think of anything that you own or control).

a. _____

b. _____

c. _____

d. _____

3. As a responsible child, what should you do when you hear the adhan?

_____

4. As a responsible child, what should you do when the Imam is talking?

_____

5. Will your responsibilities increase as you grow older?

Write Yes or No. _____

6. Are you a responsible child? Below are some of the roles for you. For each role color the choice that applies to you.

A. After dinner, :

| I put my plate in the sink | I leave my plate on the table | I ask my mom to take my plate |

B. When my clothes are dirty, I put the clothes:

In the laundry basket   On the couch   Mixed with my clean clothes

C. After I finish playing a video game:

| I leave the game on the floor | My dad cleans my mess | I clean up the game |

Obedience

Assalamu alaikum. Welcome to the class. Let us color this boy who obeys Allah (swt), and has just completed his salah.

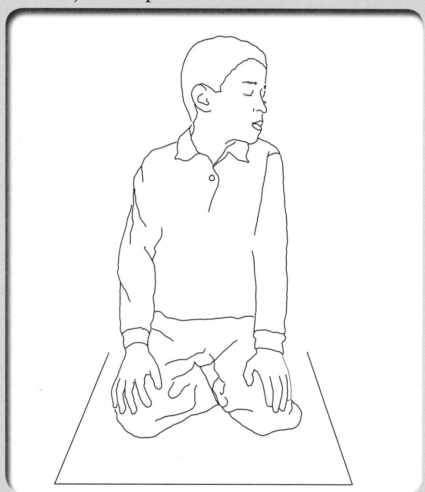

Obedience means to follow the teachings or orders of someone. Obedience is to **obey** the orders. As Muslims, we obey the orders from Allah (swt) and His Rasul (S).

Allah (swt) ordered us to make five salah every day, and He asked us to be truthful and kind. He also ordered us to follow the teachings in the Qur'an. If we listen to the orders of Allah (swt) we are **obedient** to Him. If we do not obey Allah (swt), then we are not good Muslims.

Allah (swt) also asked us to obey Rasulullah (S). Allah (swt) sent our dear Prophet Muhammad (S) to show us how to live and how to treat others. If we obey Rasulullah (S), then we are obeying Allah (swt).

Allah (swt) told us to listen to our parents. The Qur'an tells us that obedience to Allah (swt) comes first. The obedience and kindness to parents comes second. We should obey our parents, as they want the best for us. They never stop loving us. In return for their love and kindness, we have to be kind and obedient to them.

First, we obey : _____

Second, we obey our: _____

How do we obey our parents? We do not say no to them. When our parents tell us to study, it is for our **benefit**. When they call us for salah, it is for our benefit. When they tell us to go to the bed, it is for our benefit. We should not argue with them. We should not refuse to help them.

We should be good to our teachers. When we are in school, we should obey our teachers. If we do not listen to our teachers, then we cannot learn. The school has rules, so that we can learn in a safe place. We have to obey our teachers for our own benefit.

Sometimes, you may be with other older people, such as uncles, aunts or grandparents. Some of you may have older brothers or sisters. We should listen to the people who are older than us.

If you do not know someone, you have to be careful about obeying them. An **unknown** person may be good or bad. Before we listen to an unknown person, we should ask our parents.

We should never obey Shaitan. He acts as if he is our friend, but he is really our enemy. He tries to make us believe that bad things are good for us. If we obey him, then we will be in trouble. He does not want anything good for us. He is not our friend or teacher. We should never obey Shaitan.

We should obey our parents, teachers and elders. If they tell us not to listen to Allah (swt) then we need not obey them. This is because obedience to Allah (swt) comes first. We should still be kind to our parents.

Who should we never obey? _____

When can we not obey our parents? _____

_____

Words that I learned today:

Obedience • Obey • Obedient • Benefit • Unknown

1. If we do not obey Allah (swt), can we still be Muslims? Circle Yes or No.

YES   **NO**

2. Write inside the boxes any three things that Allah (swt) has told us to do.

3. What does obedience mean? (Hint: Find the answer in the first paragraph of the lesson.)

_____

_____

4. Write three ways that you were obedient to your parents this week.

a. _____

b. _____

c. _____

5.   (a) Who acts to be our friend, but is not a real friend?

_____

(b) Should we obey him?   Write Yes or No.   _____

6. Circle all the correct choices. As a good Muslim child, I obey:

Allah (swt)   Rasulullah (S)   Shaitan   Father

Mother   Grandmother   Teacher   Imam

7. Fill in the blanks using the right words:

learn   Shaitan   benefit   unknown

Salah is for our _____.

We do not obey _____.

I am careful around an _____ person.

When we obey the teacher, we _____ better.

Cleanliness

Assalamu alaikum. Welcome to the class. Let us start by coloring Jamila's bedroom. She keeps the room clean to make her salah.

Khalid and Jamilah went to their favorite playground with their parents. *"What happened to our playground? It is **littered** with empty cans, candy wrappers, and empty potato chips bags!"* Jamilah started to cry. The playground was dirty! Khalid, Jamilah and their parents joined hands to clean up the playground. Soon the playground looked clean enough to play.

Khalid and Jamilah took a shower when they went back home. They did a lot of work at the playground and needed to clean their bodies. Everyday they take shower. Nobody needs to remind them because they are responsible children. They always like to stay clean and keep things **neat** and tidy.

When it was time for Maghrib prayer, Khalid and Jamilah made wudu. Wudu prepares us to make salah. We make wudu before our salah. We must make salat on a clean place. Allah (swt) wants us to remain clean.

Khalid and Jamilah know how to make salah. They know salah should be done in a clean place. They always keep their rooms clean. They can now make salah in their rooms.

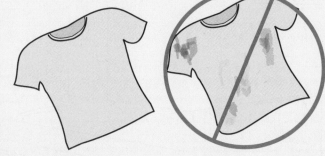

We should also wear clean clothes. Clean clothes make us feel good. We need clean clothes for making salah. When we go to the bathroom, we should make sure to keep our clothes clean. If our clothes become dirty, we have to change them. Before leaving the bathroom, we must wash our hands.

Khalid and Jamilah are good Muslims. Like all good Muslims they brush their teeth daily—after they wake up in the morning and before they go to bed. They comb and brush their hair. They always look fresh, clean and nice.

We should also wash our hands before we eat. We eat from a clean plate, and we keep our table clean. We do not want to drop food on our clothes.

We should always try to keep our minds clean. This means that we should try not to think of bad things. We should be careful about the words we use. This means that we should not use bad language when we talk to others.

Everyday, when Khalid and Jamilah read the Qur'an, they make sure that their clothes and bodies are clean. They always keep the Qur'an in a clean place, and touch the Qur'an with clean hands. In this way they show respect to the Book of Allah (swt).

> A good Muslim keeps 3 things clean. Write the names of the three things. (The first two letters are given for you)
>
> B O __ __,   C L __ __ __ __ __,   M I __ __.

This week, when Khalid and Jamilah go to the Masjid, they have a plan to clean the Masjid. They will arrange the Qur'ans on the shelves, and see if the **bulletin board** is neat. They noticed that every Muslim wears clean clothes to the Masjid, and nobody brings their shoes inside the prayer hall.

Are you a clean person? Let us find out from the following questions. Put a check mark ☑ in the box that applies to you.

	Always	Sometimes	Never
Wash your hands before eating.	☐	☐	☐
Brush your teeth everyday.	☐	☐	☐
Keep your room clean.	☐	☐	☐
Pray in a clean place.	☐	☐	☐
Keep shoes outside the prayer hall.	☐	☐	☐
Wear clean clothes.	☐	☐	☐

Words that I learned today:

Litter • Neat • Bulletin Board •

1. What do we do before making salah?

_____

2. Can we make salah when we are dirty? Circle the correct answer.

YES   NO

3. Circle the things that should be clean before we can make salah.

Body   Clothes   Prayer Rug   Bookshelf

Kitchen   Mind   Playground   Masjid

4. Circle the places that we should try to keep clean.

Bedroom   Masjid   Classroom   Playground

Living room   Kitchen   Bathroom   Backyard

Dining table   Roads   Hospital   Garden

Garage   Driveway   Neighborhood   Closet

5. Solve the crossword puzzle:

Across

1. This is the room where we sleep. We keep it clean.

2. Cleaning ourselves before making salah.

3. This is the place where we go for salah. We keep such houses clean.

Down

4. The Book of Allah (swt). We touch it with clean hands.

5. Something that covers our feet.

6. Opposite of clean.

Honesty

Assalamu alaikum. Welcome to the class. Let us color these two friends who are honestly sharing their toys.

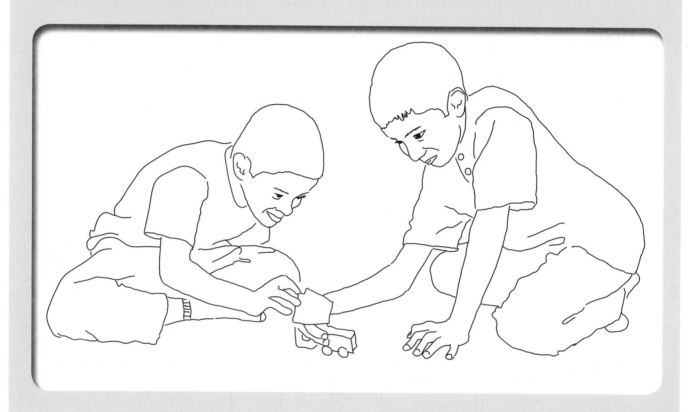

Honesty has many different meanings. One meaning is that we are true to others and also to ourselves. We are honest if we admit our mistakes. We can show honesty in two ways: (a) things that we say, and (b) things that we do.

An honest person always speaks and acts truthfully. When we do not cheat others, we are being honest. When we do not cheat or harm ourselves, we are honest to us. Honest people do not steal things even when nobody is watching them. Even if nobody is watching us, Allah (swt) always sees what we do. Allah (swt) loves an honest person.

Let us read this story, and see what we would do.

Let us say that your father left his glass of juice on the table. You were jumping around and hit the glass. The juice spilled over on the prayer rug. When your father came back, he thought that maybe the cat tipped over the glass. The cat cannot talk, so it cannot tell that you spilled the juice. What should you do? Should you say sorry and tell your father that it was not the cat?

Honesty also means that we keep our word. When we say something that we will do or not do, we should keep our word. Here is another story:

You have a nice toy that you like very much. You shared it with your friend. At first he said he would give it back to you. But he does not want to give the toy back to you. Now he is not keeping his word. How would you feel?

What are the two ways to show honesty?

(a) _____ (b) _____

When people are honest, we know we can trust them. Prophet Muhammad (S) was known as *Al-Amin*, the **trustworthy** one. People trusted him, because he never lied. We should learn from the example of our Prophet (S). Honesty means that you can be trusted.

Your neighbor asked you to pull weeds from his yard and said he would give you a nickel for each weed. After you pulled many weeds, he did not want to give you the money. Was this man being honest? Would you pull weeds for him again?

Honesty also means that we respect other's property. If something is not mine, I cannot take it secretly.

You were riding your scooter, and then came inside to pray Asr salah. When you went back out, your scooter was gone. Somebody did not respect your property—your scooter. This person was not honest. We should not take other's property, unless they want to give it to us.

Honesty is not to cheat, even if nobody is looking. Even if nobody is watching us, we should remember Allah (swt) watches us.

Who always watches everything that we do? _____

An honest person always speaks and acts: _____

You were playing a board game with a friend. You were winning the game. You went to get some cookies. When you came back, it seemed that your friend changed the dice. He was not honest; he cheated. He won the game. How would you feel? Would you play another game with this friend?

Allah (swt) told us to be honest and truthful. We should stand up for the truth. All the prophets taught us to be truthful. They did what was right, even when it was difficult.

Words that I learned today:

Honesty • Al-Amin • Trustworthy •

1. Mark with a ☑ if the sentence is correct. Mark with an ☒ if it is wrong.

Honesty is to admit our mistakes. ☐

Honesty is not to cheat. ☐

Honesty is to keep our word. ☐

Honesty is not to trust others. ☐

Honesty is to take things without asking. ☐

2. People always liked to do business with Rasulullah (S) because he was an honest, trustworthy man. Because he was trustworthy, people gave him a nice name. Can you write down the name in the space below?

_____

3. Circle **T** for true, **F** for false.

a. Honesty means being good only in the mosque. T F

b. We are honest if we tell the truth. T F

c. A Muslim should always try to be honest. T F

d. Allah (swt) loves honest people. T F

4. Suppose you found a ten dollar bill in your lunch room. Write what would you do?

_____

_____

Day of Judgment and The Hereafter

Assalamu alaikum. Welcome to the class. Let us color these fallen leaves. Like the leaves and the seasons, the world will end one day, too.

Allah (swt) is the Creator of everything. Everything that He created will come to an end one day. In spring trees are full of leaves. In autumn all the leaves fall and die. Today billions of people live on the earth. One day, all the people will also die. Only Allah (swt) lives **forever**. Nobody else lives forever. The world will not remain forever either.

After everything is destroyed, Allah will make all the dead people come back to life. The Day of **Judgment** will begin. On the Day of Judgment Allah (swt) will judge the good and bad people. Allah (swt) is the Best Judge. He will judge all our **deeds**, small and big. Nobody will be able to hide anything from Allah (swt).

Bad Deeds   Good Deeds

On the Day of Judgment, our deeds will be weighed on a **scale**. If we did more good deeds on this earth, our scale will be heavy. We will go to Heaven. If our scale is light, it will be bad for us.

Allah (swt) will call for a **witness**. A witness is someone or something that saw us doing a good or bad thing. Our bodies and things around us will tell if we did good or bad deeds. Nobody can help us if we do not do good things in this world. If we do good things, we do not have to worry about the witnesses.

The good people will have bright and happy faces. They will have nothing to fear. The bad people will have dark and sad faces. They will be very sad and ashamed that they did not follow the teachings of Allah (swt). They will want to go back to the earth to do good deeds. But they will not get a chance.

At the end of Judgment, Allah (swt) will discipline those who were evil. He will reward those who did good in this world. He will reward those who believed in Him. All good people will get their own rewards. No one can take away your rewards.

If our scale is heavy we will go to: _____

The good people will have happy _____

On the Day of Judgment, there will be three types of people. The best people will get the best rewards. The good people will be in another group who will get good rewards. The last group will be of the bad people. They will not get any rewards. They cannot borrow any reward from the good people.

After the Day of Judgment, we get another life. This is the life of the **Hereafter**. Our life on earth is short. Life in the Hereafter will last forever.

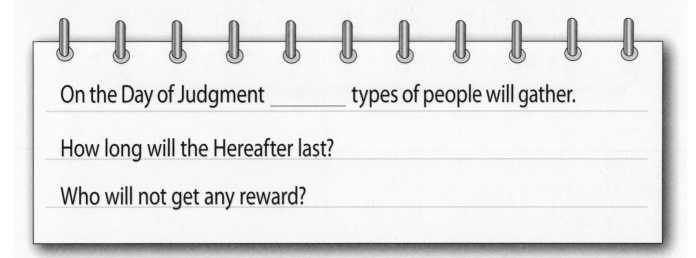

On the Day of Judgment _____ types of people will gather.

How long will the Hereafter last?

Who will not get any reward?

Allah (swt) tells us that life in the Hereafter is real. We do not know much about that life. We cannot completely understand how good that life will be. It will be better than anything that we can imagine.

If we are good Muslims, Allah (swt) will reward us with good things. The good people will be in **Jannah**, which is a beautiful Garden. This is a place of peace. Children will be together with their parents in Jannah if they were good Muslims.

Words that I learned today:

Forever • Judgment • Deeds • Scale • Witness • Hereafter • Jannah •

1. Find the following words in the puzzle.

FOREVER   JUDGMENT   SCALE
JANNAT   EARTH   REWARD   LIFE

E A R T H J A
P E R S B U N
T J E C W D W
L X W A R G P
I A A L F M R
F O R E V E R
E Q D O A N X
J A N N A T G

2. There will be three types of people on the Day of Judgment. Inside the boxes, write the three types of people.

3. What will be used to weigh our good and bad deeds? _____

4. Mark with a ☑ if the sentence is correct. Mark with an ☒ if it is wrong.

On the Day of Judgment, Allah (swt) will reward the good people. ☐

The Day of Judgment happens once every year. ☐

People can borrow rewards on the Day of Judgment. ☐

Life in the Hereafter will last for only a few years. ☐

The good people will enter Jannah, or the Garden ☐

On the Day of Judgment friends cannot help another friend. ☐

5. To get a good reward in the Hereafter, what should we do now?

_____

_____

Muslims from Different Nations

Assalamu alaikum. Can you please color this Masjid? This Masjid is in India.

When you go to your Masjid, just look around at the people. You will find that the people are from all over the world. All of them are Muslims.

You will see that some people have fair skin, and some have dark skin. The skin color maybe different, but they are all Muslim.

If you listen to the people who are talking, you will hear different languages. You will hear many people speak English. You will also hear many people speak Arabic. Some people may speak **Urdu** or **Bangla**. You may hear people talking in **Somali**, **Indonesian**, or some other languages. Muslims speak many languages, because Muslims live all over the world.

Muslims speak so many different languages, but we all learn Arabic. Allah (swt) sent us the Qur'an in Arabic. It is the most important language for Muslims. Everyday, we make our salah in Arabic.

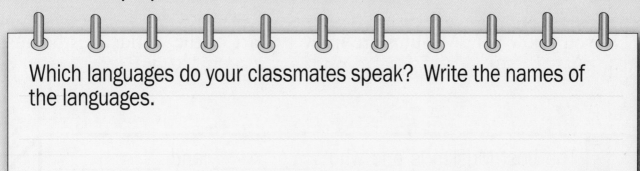

Which languages do your classmates speak? Write the names of the languages.

When you go to make Hajj, you will see that Muslims from all over the world come to Makkah. You will see people from Turkey, Iran, Malaysia, China, India, Japan and every other **nation** in the world.

Indonesia has the largest number of Muslims. Pakistan has the second largest number of Muslims. Many other countries have large numbers of Muslims. India and China are two non-Muslim countries, but have more Muslims than many Muslim countries.

Allah (swt) wants us to dress in a **modest** way. Our clothes should be clean and cover our bodies. Muslims wear different kinds of modest clothes. For example, people from Somalia wear different clothes than people from Afghanistan and Pakistan. Men from many Muslim countries wear different types of caps.

When you join an **Iftar** at a masjid, you will see that Muslims bring many kinds of foods that you may not normally eat at home. Muslims in different countries eat different foods, but all the foods are **halal**. Sometimes the foods are **spicy**, and sometimes they are sweet. We may eat any halal food.

Muslims all over the world are brothers and sisters. What we wear, how we look or what we eat do not make us better than another Muslim. The best Muslim is the one who loves Allah (swt) and obeys Him.

Do you know why Muslims are in every part of the world? It is because Allah (swt) gave Islam for all the people in the whole world!

The best Muslim is one who _____ and _____ Allah(swt).

Which country has the most Muslims? _____

Words that I learned today:

Urdu • Bangla • Somali • Indonesian • Nation • Modest • Iftar • Halal • Spicy •

1. Why do Muslims live all over the world? (Hint: Find your answer in the last paragraph of the lesson)

_____

_____

2. Mark with a ☑ if the sentence is correct. Mark with an ☒ if it is wrong.

Muslims learn Arabic because it is the language of the Qur'an. ☐

Some Muslims speak Chinese. ☐

Halal food cannot be spicy. ☐

Muslims only wear white clothes. ☐

Muslims wear clean and modest clothes. ☐

All Muslims have the same skin color. ☐

All Muslims speak the same language. ☐

3. Which two countries have more Muslims than any other country?

_____   _____

4. Do you know any Muslims who do not speak your language? If you know the names of the languages they speak, write the names in the boxes below.

5. Color the oval that has the right answer. How many people in your masjid make Salat in English?

None   About ten   About fifty

6. **extracredit.** Why do Muslims make salah in Arabic only?

_____

_____

Appendix
Steps of Salāh

Physical preparation for salāh:

Physical cleanliness: Before performing salāh, make sure you have a clean body. You must have completed *wudu*, and be in the state of *wudu*.

Clean clothes: Your clothes should be clean and should cover the body. For boys, the cloth should cover at least from the naval to the knees. For girls, the cloth should cover from the neck to the ankle, and to the wrist. The head is covered, while face can remain uncovered. Clothes should be non see-through. Avoid any clothing that has pictures of people, animals or bad writings.

Clean place: You should find a clean place to make your salāh. A prayer rug is not necessary. A prayer rug is always kept clean, and ensures a clean place when you are praying on it.

Direction: You will be facing *Qiblah*, which is the direction of Ka'bah in Makkah.

Time: *Fard* (compulsory) prayers are performed at the proper and appointed times. It is preferable to perform the prayer as soon as the *Adhan* (call to prayer) is announced or as soon as the time for salāh comes in.

Mental preparation: We will begin the prayer with full mental and physical attention. During *salāh*, we are directly talking to Allāh, therefore we must give our total attention. Avoid any place or object that can divert your attention. At no time during the salāh, should you look sideways, look at others, or talk to others in the middle of the salāh. Do not make unnecessary movements. Do not scratch, yawn, laugh or smile. If you must sneeze or cough, that is Okay, but try to minimize it.

What is a raka'ah? Each salāh can be divided into cycles of physical postures or raka'at. Each raka'ah involves the positions of *qiyam* (standing), *ruku* (bowing), *sujud* (prostration), *jalsa* (seated), and again *sujud* (prostration), all with their associated recitations. Following are the specified raka'at in the five daily salāh. Some variations on the number of Sunnah prayer exist among the madhhab.

	Sunnah raka'at before Fard raka'at	Fard raka'at	Sunnah raka'at after Fard raka'at
Fajr	2	2	
Dhuhr	4	4	2
'Asr	4	4	
Maghrib		3	2
'Isha	4	4	2, then 3 (wajib)

Description for a salāh of two raka'at:

The following description is for a salāh of two raka'at (e.g. Fard prayer of Fajr). At the end the description, there is a brief note on how to perform 3 or 4 raka'at of salāh.

Step 1 (Figures above)

Make an intention to perform the salāh for the sake of Allāh. Say to yourself (in any language) that you intend to offer this *Salāh* (*Fajr, Dhuhr, Asr, Maghrib* or *Isha*), *Fard, Sunnat* or *Witr*, and the number of raka'ahs (example—"I intend to offer two *raka'ah* of *Fard, Fajr* prayer for Allāh").

Position: *Qiyam*. You are standing upright. Raise both hands up to the ears (palms facing the *Qiblah*, —the direction to Ka'bah).

What to say: "*Allāhu Akbar*" (Allāh is the Greatest).

Step 2 (Figures on the right)

Position: Place your left hand over your stomach, and then place your right hand on top of the left hand, and grip around the wrist of the left hand.

What to say:

1. "*Subhanaka Allāhumma wa bihamdika, wa tabārakasmuka, wa ta'āla jadduka, wa lā ilāha ghairuka*". (This part is known as *thana*. It means "Glory be to you O Allāh, and praise be to You. Blessed be Your Name, exalted be Your Majesty and Glory. There is no god but You").

2. "*A'ūdu billāhi mina ash-Shaytānir rajim*" (I seek protection of Allāh against Shaitān, the condemned)

3. "*Bismillāhir rahmānir rahīm*" (In the Name of Allāh, Most Gracious, Most Merciful).

4. You will recite Sūrah Al-Fātihah now. It is a must that we recite Sūrah Al-Fātihah in each raka'ah. A salāh is not valid if Sūrah Al-Fātihah is not recited.

"*Al humdu li-llahi rabbi-l 'alamīn. Ar-rahmāni-r rahīm. Māliki yawmi-d dīn. Iyyāka na'budu wa iyyāka Nāsta'īn. Ihdina-s sirāta-l mustaqīm. Sirātal ladhīna an'amta 'alaihim, ghairil maghdūbi 'alaihim, wa la-d dāllīn. (Āmīn)*"

(The Praise belongs to Allāh, The Lord of all the worlds; the Rahman; the Rahim. Malik of the Day of Judgment. You alone do we serve, and to You alone we seek help. Guide us on the Right Path, —the path of those upon whom You have bestowed favors; not of those upon whom wrath is brought down, nor those gone-astray.)

5. After reciting sūrah Al-Fātihah, you will now recite any short sūrah or a few verses from the Holy Qur'ān. This additional recitation of a part of the Qur'ān is done in the first two raka'ah only. It is always good to memorize as many sūrah as you can, as you will recite them in your salāh.

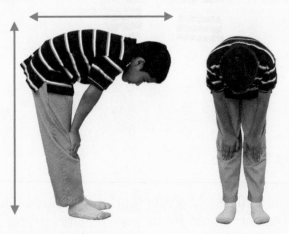

Step 3 (Figures above)

What to say: "Allāhu Akbar."

Position: This position is called ruku. Bow with your back perpendicular to your legs. Put your hands on the knees. Do not bend the knees.

What to say: "Subhana rabbiyal 'Adhīm" (say it 3 times) (Glorified is my Lord, the Great).

Step 4 (Figures below)

While going back to qiyam (upright) position,

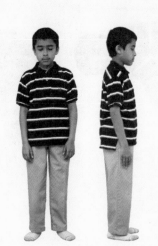

What to say: "Samia Allāhu liman hamidah" (Allāh listens to him who praises Him).

Position: In qiyam position.

What to say: "Rabbanā wa laka al hamd" ("Our Lord, praise be for You only").

Step 5 (Figure above)

What to say: While going to the next position of sujud, say "Allāhu Akbar."

Position: This position is sujud. Your will place your both knees on the floor. Try not to move the position of your feet, i.e. you will not step your feet away from the position of qiyam. After placing the knees, then you will place your two hands on the ground, with palms touching the ground. Do not glide your hands on the ground. Your elbows are away from the floor. The hands will be sufficiently apart to give space for your head. Now you will place your forehead on the floor. Both your nose and forehead should touch the floor. Your hands are on the side of your head. Your stomach will not touch the floor. You should be most humble in this position.

The most powerful part of our bodies is our brain, the site of our intelligence. We submit our full selves, with full understanding, to Almighty Allāh. We realize that our strength, power, wealth, and everything that we have is from Allāh only. To confirm this physical and spiritual humbleness, we will repeat the sujud again in Step 7.

What to say: "Subhana rabbiyal A'ala" (say it 3 times) (Glory be to Allāh, the Exalted).

Step 6 (Figures above)

The next position is *jalsa*.

What to say: While going to the *jalsa* position, say "*Allāhu Akbar.*"

Position: To go to the *jalsa* position, rise from *sujud*. First you will raise your head off the floor, then you will raise your hands. Now you are sitting on the floor, this posture is called *jalsa*.

What to say: "*Rabbi-ghfir lī wa arhamnī*" (O my Lord, forgive me and have mercy on me).

Step 7 (Figure above)

You will repeat the *sujud* again. Every *raka'ah* has two *sujud*.

What to say: While going to the position of *sujud*, say "*Allāhu Akbar.*"

Position: *Sujud.* Place your palms on the floor, then place your forehead. Both the nose and the forehead should be touching the floor.

What to say: "*Subhāna rabbiyal A'ala*" (say it 3 times) (Glory to Allāh, the Exalted").

This completes one raka'ah

Step 8 (Figures above)

You will rise to *qiyam* (upright) position. The movement should be in a systematic, graceful manner. First you will raise your forehead from the floor, then you will raise your hands off the floor, and then you will raise your knees. Try not to move your feet, i.e., the position of your feet should be in the same place as it was in the first *raka'ah*.

What to say: While going up to the position of *qiyam*, say "*Allāhu Akbar.*"

Position: You are standing upright. Hold the left hand with the right hand on top.

What to say: 1. Sūrah Al-Fātihah, and 2. Any short sūrah or some verses of the Holy Qur'ān.

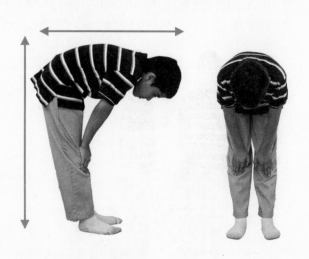

Step 9 (Figures in the previous page)

What to say: *"Allāhu Akbar."*

Position: *Ruku.* Bow with your back perpendicular to your legs. Put your hands on your knees.

What to say: *"Subhāna rabbiyal 'Adhīm"* (say it 3 times).

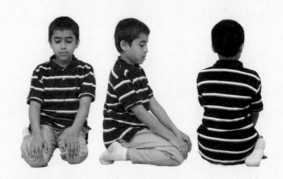

Step 12 (Figures above)

What to say: While going to the next position of *jalsa,* say *"Allāhu Akbar."*

Position: Rise from the *sujud* position. Now you are sitting in *jalsa* position.

What to say: *"'Rabbi-ghfir lī wa arhamnī"* (O my Lord, forgive me and have Mercy on me).

Step 10 (Figures above)

Position: While going back to *qiyam* (upright) position,

What to say: *"Sami'a Allāhu liman hamidah."*

Position: In *qiyam* position. You are upright.

What to say: "Rabbanā wa lakal hamd."

Step 11 (Figure below)

What to say: While going to the next position of *sujud,* say *"Allāhu Akbar."*

Position: *Sujud.* Follow the sequence as in Step 5.

What to say: *"Subhāna Rabbiyal A'ala"* (say it 3 times).

Step 13 (Figure above)

What to say: While going to the next position of sujud, say *"Allāhu Akbar."*

Position: *Sujud.* Place your hands, and then your forehead on the floor.

What to say: *"Subhāna Rabbiyal A'ala"* (say it 3 times).

Step 14 (Figures in the next page)

What to say: While going to the next position of *jalsa,* say *"Allāhu Akbar."*

Position: Rise from the *sujud* position. Now you are sitting in the *jalsa* position.

What to say: You will say the *Tashahud, Durūd* and a short prayer, as follows:

"At-tahiyātu lillahi was-salawātu wattaiyibātu. Assalāmu 'alayka ayyuhan-nabiyu wa rahmatullāhi wa barakātuhu. Assalāmu 'alainā wa 'ala 'ibadi-llāhis-sālihīn. Ashhadu an lā ilāha illallāhu wa ashhadu anna Muhammadan 'abduhu wa rasūluhu."

(All the salutations, prayers and nice things are for Allāh. Peace be on you O Prophet, and the blessings of Allāh, and His grace. Peace on us and on all the righteous servants of Allāh. I bear witness that none but Allāh is worthy of worship and bear witness that Muhammad is the servant and messenger of Allāh.) This is known as the *Tashahud*.

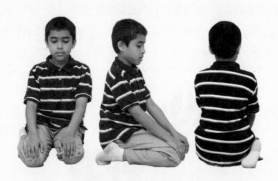

Position: raise your right index finger up while reciting the last part of this prayer.

Then you will recite the *Durūd*, (also called Salatul Ibrāhīm)

"*Allāhumma salli 'ala Muhammadin wa 'ala āli Muhummadin, kamā sallayta 'ala Ibrāhima, wa ala āli Ibrāhima, innaka hamidun majid. Allāhumma barik 'ala Muhammadin wa 'ala āli Muhummadin, kama barakta ala Ibrāhima, wa 'ala āli Ibrāhīm, innaka hamīdun majīd*".

(O Allāh, send your Mercy on Muhammad and his followers as you sent Your mercy on Ibrāhīm and his followers. You are the Most Praised, The Most Glorious. O Allāh, send your Blessings on Muhammad and his followers as you have blessed Ibrāhīm and his followers. You are the Most praised, The Most Glorious.)

You may add a short prayer, such as:

"*Rabbanā ātinā fi-d dunyā hasanatan wa fi-l ākhirati hasanatan, wa qinā 'adhāban nār*"

(Our Lord, give us the good of this world, and good in the Hereafter and save us from the chastisement of Fire.)

Step 15 (Figure above left)

Position: Slowly turn your face to the right. This is called *Taslim*.

What to say: "*As-salāmu 'alaikum wa rahmatullāh*" (Peace and mercy of Allāh be on you).

Step 16 (Figure above right)

Position: Slowly turn your face to the left. This is called *Taslim*.

What to say: "*As-salāmu 'alaikum wa rahmatullāh*."

This completes the two raka'at of salāh.

How to pray three raka'ats (Maghrib)

In order to perform a three raka'at Salāh, all the postures and the prayers are the same up to step 13. But this time in step 14, recite only *"At-tahiyātu lillahi was-salawātu wattaiyibātu. Assalāmu 'alayka ayyuhan-nabiyu wa rahmatullāhi wa barakātuhu. Assalāmu 'alainā wa 'ala 'ibadi-llāhis-sālihīn. Ashhadu an lā ilāha illallāhu wa ashhadu anna Muhammadan 'abduhu wa rasūluhu."* This is known as *Tashahud*.

Saying *Allāhu akbar,* return back to the *qiyam* position, step 8. This time recite only *Al-Fātihah,* (in step 8). There is no recitation of any sūrah or part of the Holy Qur'ān. Then all prayers and postures are the same as shown from step 9 - 16.

How to pray four raka'ats (Dhuhr, 'Asr and 'Isha)

In order to perform a four raka'at prayer, all the postures and the prayers are the same up to step 13.

In Step 14 only the prayer of *"Tashahud"* will be recited, and the *qiyam* position, step 8, will be resumed.

In position 8 only *Al-Fātihah,* will be recited without adding any sūrah. Step 8 - 13, completes the fourth raka'ah. The *qiyam* position, step 8, will be re-assumed.

In position 8 only *Al-Fātihah,* will be recited without adding any sūrah. Step 8 - 16, completes the fourth raka'ah.

From the Qur'an

...keep up the salat, as salah controls indecent and unacceptable behaviors... *(Surah Al-Ankabut, 29:45)*

Take care to make your salah, praying in the best way, and stand before Allah with full devotion. *(Surah Al-Baqarah, 2:238)*

Outline of Curriculum – Grades 1, 2 and 3

Every year the curriculum begins with a few topics on Allāh, the Qur'ān, the Prophet (S), and the Hadīth or Sunnah. In the early years, the emphasis is placed on the 5-pillars, and each year, the emphasis increases. Every year the history of some of the prophets is introduced in an age appropriate manner. Each year, several lessons are devoted to Islamic values to make the children grow up with a good understanding of Islamic manners, values and morals. All the lessons are followed by homework.

Week	1st Grade	2nd Grade	3rd Grade
1	Allāh	Allāh the Creator	What Does Allāh Do
2	Islam	Blessings of Allāh	Some Names of Allāh
3	Our Faith	The Qur'ān	Allāh : The Merciful
4	Muhammad (S)	Muhammad (S)	Allāh : The Judge
5	Qur'ān	Sunnah and Hadīth	We are Muslims
6	Exam is recommended in this week		
7	5 Pillars of Islam	5 Pillars of Islam	Other Names of the Qur'ān
8	Shahādah	Shahādah	Hadith
9	Salāh and Wūdū	Salāt	Shahādah
10	Fasting	Sawm	Types of Salāh
11	Zakāh	Charity	Why to do Salāh
12	Exam is recommended in this week		
13	Hajj	Hajj	Sawm
14	Saying "Bismillāh"	Wūdū	Charity
15	Angels	Four Khalīfas	Hajj
16	Shaitān	Ibrāhīm (A)	Prophet (S) in Makkah
17	Adam (A)	Ya'qūb (A) and Yūsuf (A)	Prophet (S) in Madinah
18	Nūh (A)	Mūsā (A) and Harun (A)	How Rasul (S) treated others
19	Exam is recommended in this week		
20	Ibrāhīm (A)	Yūnus (A)	Ismā'īl (A) and Ishāq (A)
21	Mūsā (A)	Angels	Dāwūd (A)
22	'Isā (A)	Foods That Ee May Eat	'Isā (A)
23	Makkah and Madinah	Truthfulness	Being Kind
24	Good Manners	Kindness	Forgiveness
25	Kindness and Sharing	Respect	Good Deeds
26	Exam is recommended in this week		
27	Allāh Rewards Good Works	Responsibility	Cleanliness
28	Respect	Obedience	Right Path
29	Forgiveness	Cleanliness	Muslim Family
30	Love of Allāh	Honesty	Perseverance
31	Eid	Day of Judgment and Hereafter	Punctuality
32	Thanking Allāh	Muslims from Different Nations	Jinn
33	Exam is recommended in this week		

Outline of Curriculum – Grades 4, 5 and 6

By 5th grade a summarized biography of the Prophet (S) is completed with an understanding of events that shaped his life and early Islam. By 6th grade, the students will have studied the biography of most of the prominent prophets at least once. By now the students will have learned all the fundamental principles and all key concepts of Islam. Even if the students do not come back to weekend schools after 6th grade, they still will have gained significant age-appropriate knowledge about Islam.

Week	4th Grade	5th Grade	6th Grade
1	Rewards of Allāh	Allāh Our Sole Master	Attributes of Allāh
2	Discipline of Allāh	Why Should We Worship Allāh	Promise of Allāh
3	Some Names of Allāh	Revelation of the Qur'ān	Objective of the Qur'ān
4	Books of Allāh	Characteristics of Prophets	Compilation of the Qur'ān
5	Pre-Islamic Arabia	Battle of Badr	Previous Scriptures and the Qur'ān
6	Exam is recommended in this week		
7	The Year of the Elephant	Battle of Uhud	Importance of Shahādah
8	Early Life of Muhammad (S)	Battle of Trench	Hadīth, Compilation, Narrators
9	Life before Prophethood	Hudaibiyah Treaty	Nūh (A)
10	Receipt of Prophethood	Conquest of Makkah	Talut, Jalut and Dāwūd (A)
11	Makkan Period	Adam (A)	Dāwūd (A) and Sulaimān (A)
12	Exam is recommended in this week		
13	Pledges of Aqaba	Ibrāhīm (A) and His Arguments	Sulaimān (A) and Queen of Saba
14	Hijrat to Madinah	Ibrāhīm (A) and Idols	Mūsā (A) and Fir'awn
15	Madīnan Period	Luqmān (A) and His Teachings	Israelites After Their Rescue
16	Victory of Makkah	Yūsuf (A) – Childhood and Life in Aziz's Home	Mūsā (A) and Khidir
17	Abū Bakr (R)	Yūsuf (A) – Life in Prison and his Dream Interpretation	'Isā (A) and Maryam (ra)
18	'Umar al-Khattāb (R)	Yūsuf (A) - Dream Fulfills	Khadījah (ra)
19	Exam is recommended in this week		
20	'Uthmān ibn 'Affan (R)	Ayyūb (A)	'A'ishah (ra)
21	'Ali Ibn Abu Tālib (R)	Zakariyyāh (A) and Yahyā (A)	Fātimah (ra)
22	Compilers of Hadīth	Maryam	Awakening
23	Shaitān's Mode of Operation	Major Masjid in the World	Rūh and Nafs
24	Hūd (A)	Upholding Truth	Angel and Jinn
25	Sālih (A)	Responsibility and Punctuality	Shaitān's Strategy
26	Exam is recommended in this week		
27	Mūsā (A)	My mind, My Body	Taqwā
28	Sulaimān (A)	Kindness and Forgiveness	My Friend is Muslim Now
29	Truthfulness	Middle Path	Friendship with Others / with Opposite Gender
30	Perseverance	Significance of Salāt	Reading salāh vs Performing Salāh
31	Day of Judgment	Significance of Fasting	Muslims Around the World
32	'Eid and its Significance	Zakāt and Sadaqah - Significance	People of Other Faiths
33	Exam is recommended in this week		

Outline of Curriculum – Grades 7, 8 and 9

The application of knowledge is gradually emphasized through carefully selected topics. Details about some of the prophets are introduced to highlight the abiding moral in their lives. In 8th grade several battles and early Muslim struggles are discussed in detail. Depth and emphasis in the lessons require increased attention from the students. Age appropriate moral lessons, e.g. gossip, friendship, peer pressure, dating, indecency, enjoining good and forbidding evil, etc. are covered.

Week	7th Grade	8th Grade	9th Grade
1	Why Islam, What is Islam	Divine Names	Signs of Allāh in Nature
2	The Qur'ān - Other Names	Objective of the Qur'ān	Ponder Over the Qur'ān
3	Seeking Forgiveness of Allah - Istighfar	Hadīth	Preservation and Compilation of the Qur'ān
4	Allāh: Angry or Kind	Madhhab	Ibadat - Some Easy Ways to do it
5	Islamic Greetings	Hope, Hopefulness, Hopelessness	Why Human Beings are Superior
6	Exam is recommended in this week		
7	Adam (A)	Trial	Is Islam a Violent Religion
8	'Ad and Thamūd	Friends and Friendship	Peer pressure
9	Stories of Ibrāhīm (A)-I	Friendship with Non-Muslims	Choices We Make
10	Stories of Ibrāhīm (A) -II	Dating in Islam	Dating in Islam
11	Sacrifice of Ibrāhīm (A)	Duties Towards Parents	Alcohol and Gambling
12	Exam is recommended in this week		
13	Lūt (A)	Islam for Middle School Student	Permitted and Prohibited Foods
14	Yūsuf (A)- Story of Overcoming temptation	Battle of Badr	Food of the People of the Book
15	Dwellers of Cave	Battle of Uhud	Khadījah (ra)
16	Dhul Qurnain	Banu Qaynuka	Prophet's Multiple Marriages
17	Abū Sufyān	Banu Nadir	Marriage with Zainab (ra)
18	Khālid Ibn Walīd (R)	Battle of Khandaq	The Prophet: A Great Army General
19	Exam is recommended in this week		
20	How to Achieve Success	Banu Qurayzah	God's Chosen People
21	Character of the Prophets	Surah Al-Ahzāb on the Battle of Khandaq	Mūsā's Personality
22	Prophet's Marriages	Hudaibiyah Treaty	Prophecy of Muhammad(S) in Bible
23	Purification	Tabūk Expedition	Shī'ah Muslims
24	Permitted and Prohibited	Farewell Pilgrimage	Muslims in North America
25	Lailatul Qadr	Performance of Hajj	Life Cycle of Truth
26	Exam is recommended in this week		
27	Fasting in Ramadan	Paradise and Hell	How Ramadan Makes us Better
28	My Family is Muslim Now	Finality of Prophethood	Indecency
29	Amr Bil Ma'rūf	Origin and History of Shī'ah	Allegations Against the Prophet (S)
30	Guard Your Tongue	Ummayad Dynasty	Family Values
31	Lessons From Past Civilizations	Abbasid Dynasty	Shariah
32	Science in the Qur'ān	Permitted and Prohibited Foods	Justice in Islam
33	Exam is recommended in this week		

Outline of Curriculum – Grades 10, 11 and 12

In 10th, 11th and 12th grades, the topics increasingly prepare the youths to fine tune their young-adult lives. More serious issues are introduced that have real life implications. The application of knowledge continues to be emphasized. Age appropriate moral lessons, like righteousness in Islam, marriage, dowry issues, the divorce process, music in Islam, and jihād etc. are introduced.

Week	10th Grade	11th Grade	12th Grade
1	History of Allāh	"Discovering" God	Our God, Their God
2	An Analysis of Fātiha	Kalam of Allāh	Loving Allāh
3	Fātiha vs. Lord's Prayer	Precedence of Mercy in Allāh	Literal Interpretation of the Qur'ān
4	Muhkam Mutashabihat Verses	Importance of the Qur'ān in Life	Management 101 - from the Prophet's Life
5	Being Khalifa on the Earth	Succession to Muhammad (S)	Apostasy
6	Exam is recommended in this week		
7	False Piety	Victory Comes from Apparent Setback	Husband and Wife - Garment for Each Other
8	The Bible and the Qur'ān	Accountability	Dowry Process
9	Adam and Eve in the Garden	Righteousness in Islam	Divorce Process
10	The Ten Commandments and Islam	10 years of Life Changing Foundation	Lian Verses
11	Racism in Islam	Light upon the Light	Hijab Verses
12	Exam is recommended in this week		
13	Superstition	Ruh, Nafs, Spirit, Bodies	Marital Relations of the Prophet (S)
14	Al-Asr - Timing of the Day	Responsibilities in Married Life	Men are Head of Household
15	Position of Women in Islam	Divorce	Flogging an Adulterer
16	Marriage with Non-Muslims	Balancing Faith Amid Diversity	Why Two Women Witness
17	Distinctive Females in Qur'ān	Importance of Keeping the "Trust"	Hur in Heaven
18	Women's Rights in Islam	Music in Islam	Is Islam a Violent Religion
19	Exam is recommended in this week		
20	Establishing Salāh: Institutionalize It	Fitra - Innate Human Nature	Jihād Verses
21	Goodly Loan	Heedlessness in Human Being	Hajj: Understanding the Significance
22	Fiqh	Importance of Tolerance	"Beating thy Wife"
23	Death	Guidance and Misguidance	"Part time Muslim"
24	Do Not Transgress Limites	Stages of Life and Death	Muslim Youths in the US
25	Public Finance in Early Islam	This World and the Next World	MSA - An Introduction
26	Exam is recommended in this week		
27	Business Ethics	How to Enjoy Life Islamic way	Islamophobia: How to Deal with it
28	Balance in Life	Wrongdoings - How to Identify and Avoid Them	Future Muslims
29	Islam in America	How to Pray Janaza Prayer	Independent project
30	Islam in India	Understanding Judaism	Independent project
31	Islam in Spain	Judaism, Christianity and Islam	Independent project
32	Islam in Turkey	Dependence, Independence	Independent project
33	Exam is recommended in this week		

Other Useful Books from weekendLearning

Arabic Writing Workbook

128 pages

Teaches students how to write Arabic with easy to follow instructions. Practice letters are given in shaded form, followed by blank lines to polish writing skills. Plenty of pages for year long writing practice.

My Islamic Coloring Book

136 pages $10.00

Give your child the head start he/she deserves. By completing this coloring and activity book, your child will gain introduction to Islam and progress to the next level of learning. The book has 14 different activities.

Coloring Allah's names ● Coloring things Allah created ● Coloring Islamic phrases ● Coloring Arabic alphabets ● Coloring Arabic numbers ● Coloring books of Allah ● Coloring 5-pillars of Islam ● Coloring prophets names ● Coloring Khalifa's names ● Coloring salat steps ● Coloring zakat activity ● Coloring Hajj activity ● Coloring family values ● Fun and learning activities

Quiz Book on Islam for All Levels of Expertise (2nd ed.)

By Husain A. Nuri

160 pages $10.00

Written by Quiz Master of an Interstate Quiz Bowl. The book is designed to boost Children's Islamic knowledge. Even adults will enjoy the book. The book has over 1,700 questions covering more than 100 different topics. The questions are divided into basic, intermediate and advanced sections. Each page has 15–17 questions. Many questions have explanatory answers. Turn to this book to quickly learn a variety of facts about Islam.

Juz 'Amma for School Students

By Husain A. Nuri and Mansur Ahmad

216 pages $12.00

The book is a student friendly presentation of the 30th Part of the Qur'an. The book contains large and clear Arabic text, transliterations and translations in a three-column format. Each sūrah starts with an introduction, followed by explanation of the verses. A "word to know" section provides root and derivatives of several key words. This is followed by a word-to-word meaning of the entire sūrah. Each chapter ends with some teachings in the sūrah that the children can apply in their everyday lives. A short question section reinforces the materials learned.